DORIE and PEGGY

Homecoming---

Peggy, the stroke survivor. Jan '97

compose a song of praise to it); and of the
practical advantages of friendship with Roberta.

Peggy and Roberta pioneer with their heady
adventures into Portland's forbidden wilderness
spots as well as a playful world of words. Dorie
discovers a hidden talent, and Peggy refuses to
discover something about Dorie.   Money
problems lead to Black Friday.

Peggy and Roberta go to Camp Namanu.   On
their first day home, Peggy acts badly (like an
editor) in Sunday school; the new teacher
devastates the family with a decision.   When
further devastation comes from a Sunday in the
park, Peggy finds comfort in her hoard of
Webster's treasures.

Winding up the Portland era, this chapter takes
Peggy through her turbulent teens, the gain and
loss of another best friend, the war years, and at
last to the discovery of a thrilling trinity: the
dictionary, the typewriter, and the lone
Adventurer.

CONTENTS
AND
CHAPTER SUMMARIES

Peggy explains that her story, although based on childhood memories, is partly a product of her imagination.

Worried because her little sister Dorie seems to have stopped growing, Peggy looks for help from a teacher of health. Although she doesn't quite tumble to the fact that health is a euphemism for manners, her healing quest leads her to Webster's, through the booby traps of sassing, and straight into a spanking.

A bumbler in sports, Peggy shines in spelling bees and wins a championship in a family word game. After Sunday school, she and Dorie enter into a secret life with Roberta and her sister Noreen. With the help of Webster's, she begins to probe the mysteries of sex and discovers something she'd rather not know about her father's profession.

Peggy gets her first taste of glamour–Roberta's birthday party; of the power of demeaning words (neutralized by Webster's, inspiring her to

DORIE and PEGGY

by

Peggy Brandstrom Pavel

For Ele & Ken,
with love & fond
memories over the years,
from Peggy (posthumously)
and Victor

Honolulu, Valentine's Day, 2001

ISBN: 1-58820-348-4

This book is printed on acid free paper.

1stBooks - rev. 12/26/00

*This book is dedicated to Dorie
and all the members of her D.S. Family*

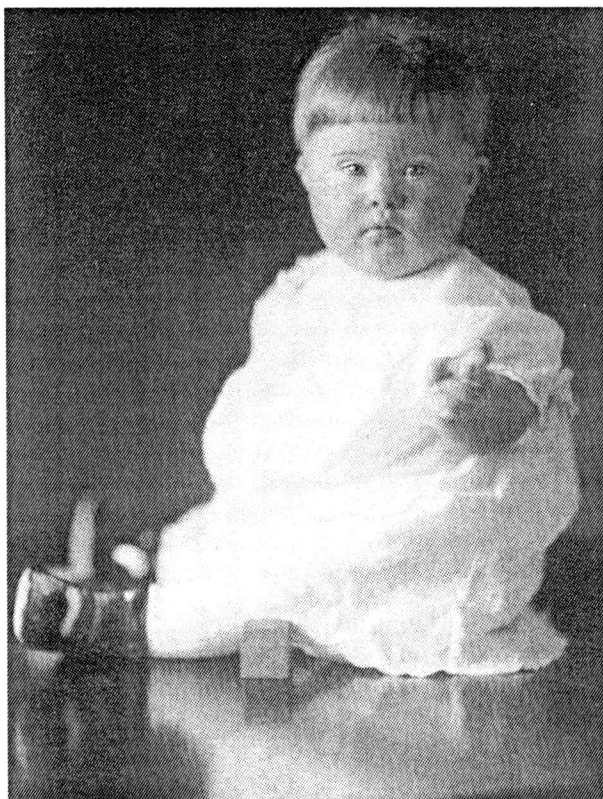

Dorothy Anne Brandstrom 1924-1992

*The author is donating 100% of her book royalties to
National Down Syndrome Society*

Here Peggy finally focuses on Dorie, who seldom shows up in this summary because most of the action flows freely around her. But she's a haunting presence in the book, so in this epilogue Peggy uncovers the tragedy her young eyes didn't let her see: Down's Syndrome.

Victor's postscript–handed to Peggy as notes he hoped she'd incorporate in her writing–shows him establishing a posthumous rapport with a sister-in-law he knew for thirty years but with whom he never exchanged a single word.

TRUE OR FALSE?

No one who goes back sixty years to look at her world with childhood eyes can claim she's dealing only with fact. Memory blurs, colors, and erases many details. When memory falters, imagination kicks in, because the very act of putting words on paper produces its own stagelike reality. The scenery appears, characters come forward, events unfold, dialog springs into life.

Except for my family, my "remembered" characters (their names changed) and some events evolved in an enchanted Oregon forest of my own creation. But as Aesop proved, the fact that imagination plays a part doesn't make a story untrue. And there really was a Mrs. Chumley...who might not recognize herself as the person who continues to instruct and inspire in my grateful memory.

I.
LITTLE LESSONS

"Ach, Axel. Do something about the flicka."

When Grandpa Brandstrom said that to Daddy about me, he meant "Shut her up." When he said it about my little sister Dorie, he meant "Get her out of my sight." Although he lived with us for a month or two each year, he never once pretended to like either of us. Fat and red-faced, he wore a gold watch chain across his vest that jiggled when he walked, a mustache over his lips that jiggled when he talked. He didn't walk much but he talked all the time; and heaven help us if we didn't listen to every word, even when he growled out whole sentences in Swedish.

"But why do I have to keep quiet?" I whined to Mother as we did the dinner dishes.

<u>Finally</u> did them. Night after night, Grandpa kept us at the table while he drank coffee and delivered a sermon heaving with Jehovah's glory, Satan's flames, and sinful, backsliding children. Through his standing orders, Dorie had to disappear when the dessert plates did, and I could neither leave nor talk.

"And why can't Dorie stay at the table with us? Whose house is this anyway?"

Once in a while Mother sympathized. "I know, Peggy," she'd sigh. "It's hard on us all." Sometimes she tried to help me understand. "We have to show him respect -- to be patient for Daddy's sake." Less often, and far better, she let her own fury show, tossing silverware around with a fine fearless clanging clatter. "Because that's life. When Grandpa's here he rules the roost." But usually she crimped her lips, shook her head, and cut me off. "Don't argue, miss. You have lots more to learn than you have to say, and don't you dare forget it."

Why was "Why?" always an argument -- not a fair question?

One awful night Grandpa threw his fork across the table at Dorie, banishing her before she finished her cake.

"OUT!" he yelled "OUT OUT OUT OUT!"

1

She went quietly, and I sat quietly until I carried off the dishes. Then I let my argument fly -- by smashing his sticky plate on the kitchen floor.

"Grandpa's an evil tyrant," I bellowed, rejoicing in the mess, the noise, the strange gleam in Mother's eyes.

"Shush now, child."

"Dorie doesn't either mess up her food. She just likes to play with it for a little bit. He's the sloppy one."

It was true. Grandpa, gesturing wildly as he spouted about sin, always spilled crumbs and gravy on the tablecloth. Dorie ate slowly, took the time to admire each forkful. Concentrating, she might bury each string bean deep in her mashed potatoes, then laugh with each unearthing; or carve a winding road up her ice cream mountain; or, as she had that night, cut her cake into twelve pieces to arrange around the rim of her plate. "Doh makes a clock," she announced, then chimed like our hall one as she ate each hour. How could anyone resist chiming right along with her?

"Mother, it wasn't fair. He should have banished me too. And what if his fork had hit her?" I blew out my cheeks, planted my fists on my hips, ready for whatever punishment came. "Grandpa's nothing but a wicked old ogre."

"Shush, dear. Don't let them hear you," Mother whispered, sweeping up my mess.

It was the "dear" that did it. I burst into tears, howling, "Mama, he has no right! Dorie's ours!" To my horror, Mother dropped the broom and sank to the floor with me in her lap.

What on earth had I done? I wondered, terrified by her wrenching sobs, hurting from the pressure of her arms, our out-of-sync spasms. Could we ever stop crying? As we slowed down a familiar splutter from Grandpa came through the door: "The barn smakan for a spanken." I knew I was the barn he meant, but Mother did all the spanking in our house, and she was busy -- too busy, even, for us to do the dishes as usual while the coffee perked.

Centuries and centuries later, she took a deep, shuddering breath, pulled us up to our feet, wiped both of our faces.

"Don't you ever let me catch you getting schnoor on a dishtowel again," she said, half laughing. "Now get out there. Go be civil to that mean old tyrant while I do the coffee."

"Daddy should defend his castle." I had to make sure my voice still worked.

"That's enough from you," she said, pushing me through the swinging door. That's more like it, I thought, relieved to get back the no-nonsense mother I knew best. A few minutes later when Daddy winked across the table I even managed to wink back.

Mother sometimes wound Grandpa down by moving him out of hell-fire and into the Old Country; during a pause, she'd excuse me and I could finally escape -- often past bedtime.

"Pah's here," Dorie murmured from her bed in the semidarkness, a sitting Buddha silhouetted against the venetian blinds. Already in her pajamas, she padded behind me into the bathroom to perch on the edge of the tub while I changed into mine -- hurriedly, so we wouldn't cross Grandpa's path as he came up to bed.

Because his room was next to ours, we didn't dare tell stories or sing ourselves to sleep; we could only hold hands across the beds as Dorie whispered her nightly litany.

"Mah okay? Dah okay? Gahpah okay?" As I grunted my third "Mmmm" I crossed my fingers on the hand Dorie couldn't feel. "Then Pah and Doh okay."

She nestled down, content; I settled in to welcome my fairy godmother, or a good witch, or Punjab, or a genie, or maybe even a special angel from a nicer God than Grandpa's. Each night of Grandpa's visit, one of them swooped into Portland to rescue us all by whisking him, surprised speechless, back to Sweden or down to China or off to a far corner of the moon....

The day Grandpa left -- by morning train to Aunt Gertrude in Seattle -- always sparkled with back-to-normal treats for us all.

Mother put on lipstick the minute our car went down the driveway, sang "Happy Days Are Here Again" over the whir of the vacuum cleaner. Dorie, dizzy with freedom, switched the radio from one station to another, dancing for as long as she pleased. Daddy came in whistling at five o'clock, a big grin on his face and a cigarette in his hand; the smoke, sweeter than roses, chased out the sour leftovers of Grandpa's turpentine and oil paint that drifted up from the basement. ("At least when he paints he's out of my hair for a while," I'd heard Mother tell Daddy. "His paints and canvases are expensive but they're worth every dime.") Dinner felt like a party, bubbling with our own noise and dear old jokes. Out from under the clickety-clack of Grandpa's dentures, Mother always celebrated by serving steak.

"Will you say grace, dear?" she asked Daddy as she brought it to the table.

"Grace dear, but it's you I love, Anna darling."

"Amen and dig in!" I shouted, and even Mother and Daddy knew nothing was ever funnier.

Best of all, we finished the dishes by seven. Dorie and I ran out whooping like Indians on the warpath to play with the neighborhood kids until dark. Most of us lived on Couch Street's 3500 block: Harriet McKay and little Herbie from across the street; Alice Dole from next door; the three Vlahos boys from one corner, Irene and Jimmy Caspar from the other; and the come-and-go children from two rental houses. Others from nearby blocks strayed in regularly and so did a few teens and near-teens. Eleanor Holden told us stories. Billie Birch liked to referee. The Dailey boys, pretending to be cowboys on horses, circled us on bikes, rounding us up for slaughter.

(Why did none of my classmates ever join us? I wondered. Two of them, Mitzi and Daniel, lived on the 3500 block of Burnside, too busy a street to play on; and one, the mysterious Roberta Northrup -- Queen Roberta -- lived on Ankeny, in a huge house right behind Daniel's. Well, it's their loss, I decided every time Mitzi and Daniel flitted by on bikes, but I longed for them to stay; I wanted to pump Daniel about Roberta. I'd never set eyes on her outside of school, and she talked only to the teachers. Her house, a fortress of gray stone behind thick, unfriendly hedges, was as forbidding as she was; I spied on it from the street side whenever I could. Was she a prisoner in there? Did Daniel, across the fence, ever see anything suspicious? Ever wake up to screams in the night?)

In midsummer, it was light until almost ten o'clock -- past bedtime for most of us. As darkness closed in our parents, like alert cuckoos, popped out onto porches to whistle us home. We knew each other's distinctive whistles, and the difference in tempo between "It's almost bedtime" and "Get in or get smacked."

When it grew too dark to play in the street, and all winter, we played in a front yard -- usually Alice's or mine, because houses on our side sat high on a grassy slope, a perfect setting for king of the mountain and statue, or a comfortable backrest if we settled down for ghost stories. The driveways' central steps were ideal for top of the class, a game we might have made up. "Kee-rect," the teacher would say. "Pro-ceed upward one level," and up one step the smart one inched -- on his haunches, backwards, with no hands, to make it tough going.

Butter-fingered, clumsy, as soft and bruisable as a banana, I liked the yard games best; in the street games, Dorie and I were always chosen last, to fill as a pair such unpopular positions as pigtail or keeper of the can. Then one day, right in the middle of a scrimmage, Dorie quit, choosing instead to sit on the curb as our cheering section. "Doh's too small," she said, puzzled.

And suddenly she was. Even little Herbie, a year younger, was bigger than she was. Had she shrunk overnight?

It puzzled me too, but who could help me? Not Mother, who wouldn't allow certain kinds of questions. I'd learned that the hard way when I asked why Dorie didn't start kindergarten when she was five, as I had. Mother wheeled on me, as red-faced as Grandpa, and gave me a stinging slap on my bottom. "You just tend to your own knitting, miss. Do you hear me? And if others ask you why, you tell them to tend to their own knitting too."

"Others" didn't worry me; Dorie did. What could I tell her when she asked from her bed when she'd be big enough to go to school too?

She asked it more often after she stopped playing the street games. It was getting harder to satisfy her with "We have our own private school at home," though that always brought a smile; she loved the rainy afternoons when she and I played school in the kitchen nook. Once in a while I was the auditorium teacher, showing how to pledge allegiance, bring the meeting to order, second the motion. Sometimes I was Miss Hoag, teaching arithmetic. Most of the time I was Mrs. Adams, spelling out in block letters each new word. Mother, puttering around the kitchen, occasionally dropped in as the principal, and kept us in an endless supply of magic slates. "That should make it a game for you too," she said, with her you're-a-good-big-sister smile.

Dorie was always me: paying attention, sitting up straight, minding her manners, showing respect, and keeping a civil tongue in her head. Whenever we got to sentences she decided it was more fun to draw. THIS IS THE HOUSE THAT DORIE DREW, I wrote. She copied the letters, sounded out the words, and proclaimed proudly that "Doh knows how to read and write." Then she snapped it out to start another picture. "Time for art class now."

Could I ask Harriet's mother if she knew why Dorie had stopped growing? Mrs. McKay really liked Dorie; she was the only neighborhood mother who ever invited Dorie without me -- to go to a matinee with Herbie, or to picnic in the park, or to come over to play on a rainy day. But mothers tattled. Even asking Harriet to ask her mother might he smakan for a spanken.

Mitzi could help; Mitzi knew everything. If only I could make friends with her ... but that was asking for worse than a spanking. ("Too much for her own good is what she knows," said Mother, grim. "She'd bring out the worst in you, so you stay away from her.") Even so: I knew that Mitzi, her pockets always jingling with nickels and pennies, showed up often at the drugstore at Thirty-second and Burnside, so for many weeks I did too.

At the January assembly we met a new teacher -- of health. My third-grade section would meet with her every Monday after lunch. Oh thank you God, I sighed. A thousand thanks. A health teacher was bound to know how to start Dorie growing again.

Mrs. Chumley was short and squarish, with short, gray, bristly hair; her glasses kept falling off her nose to bobble on her chest like a necklace. She paced up and down the aisles, stopping often to shake a finger in the nearest face. Because she made us stand up when spoken to, we jumped up and down a lot.

And over the weeks she had a lot to say.

"Little Pitchers, cover your mouth when you find it necessary to yawn. Do you ever yawn in public, Lillian? No? Nonsense. You were doing it just now."

"Little Pitchers, do you know why I call you that? Frances? Benjamin? I did not think so. I call you that to remind you that little pitchers have big ears, and I expect you to utilize your ears fully in my class. Big ears and small mouths -- those are the materials from which good children are made."

"A good child is never bored. Betsy, do you ever complain to your mother, 'Poor me. I have nothing to do'? For shame if you say yes, and I do not believe it if you say no. Do you know what boredom indicates, Charles? No? It proves you are woefully neglecting your mental resources, ignoring your hidden potential."

"A hiccough is a spasm, just as a cough is. Remember cough when you think of hiccough, because it will help your spelling. Pick up your pencils and write this down: h-i-c-c-o-u-g-h. You might see it spelled h-i-c-c-u-p in your disgraceful comic books, or even in the dictionary. Even though the dictionary spells it both ways, you must not assume that both versions are correct. One spelling is vulgar, the other is genteel."

After school we often made fun of her, shaking our fingers and calling each other little pitchers. Secretly I looked forward to her class, and brought a special notebook for new words. No other teacher used such big ones, or ever hinted that it was possible to argue with the dictionary. Her big words seemed a gift especially for me, because at Christmas Daddy had proudly brought home a for-the-family present: a Webster's dictionary, so big that it sat on its own stand under the window in the den.

"I'm still learning English," he said, explaining that since he'd spent his childhood in Sweden he had a lot of catching up to do. "I learn twenty new words a day."

He started to give me an arithmetic problem -- how long would it take him to learn all six hundred thousand words? -- but I headed that off. "Can I learn twenty words a day instead?"

He laughed. "Well, I'm going through it alphabetically; you probably wouldn't want to do that for very long. So why don't you collect new words that you come across -- say twenty a week. I'll test you on them at our Sunday night games. Okay?"

So in class I sat with pencil poised for new words, ears open for clues on how to help Dorie start growing again.

"Little Pitchers, here are the rudiments of good manners: Listen to what adults say. Daniel, what did I just say? You do not know? Rude little boys don't listen. Mitzi, what did I say?"

"That Daniel's a rude little boy."

"For shame, Mitzi. You are a rude little girl and you will come in after school to repair your manners. You too, Daniel."

"A well-bred child always carries a clean handkerchief. Girls, if you tell everyone how much you cherish a prettily embroidered handkerchief, you will be gratified at how quickly you will accumulate an imposing collection. Roberta, let me see yours. I knew it -- tidily folded in your purse"

She asked Roberta to walk up and down the aisles so everyone could admire her handkerchief. Didn't Roberta ever smile? Or ever frown? Had somebody drugged her?

"Thank you, Roberta. You are indeed a refined little lady, as your handkerchief proves. Charles, show me yours. I expected as much -- all wadded up in your pocket. For shame."

On the next Monday she brought an iron and ironing board, to show us how to form handkerchiefs into rectangles, triangles, double triangles, accordion pleats.

"Little Pitchers, I beseech you to show loving respect for your mothers by learning how to iron your own. And show respect for your handkerchiefs too. Never debase them by calling them hankies. That term is slang, a crudity that is below the dignity of ladies and gentlemen."

8

Maybe ironing hankies was important, but.... In March I told Harriet that helping Dorie grow wasn't going to be as easy as I'd hoped. "Mrs. Chumley doesn't say much about health."

"Why not ask the school nurse? Or I can ask Mother if --"

"No, please. Not yet. A health teacher has to get around to health sometime, doesn't she?"

Sometimes Mrs. Chumley really surprised me. "Little Pitchers, this is important: Cry when you are spanked," she said one day. I sat up straight to listen. Was there a choice?

"You must cry to show your parents that you are sincerely repentant and have willingly learned your lesson. Frances, what important rule of behavior did I just impart?"

"That I must cry when my parents spank me to show them I've learned my lesson. I always do, Mrs. Chumley, and so does my best friend Betsy Baum."

"You are well-behaved daughters. To be a well-behaved child you must remember this: Just as your parents have the beholden duty to prepare you for life, you have the beholden duty to cooperate with them."

"Little Pitchers, give your seat on the bus to the elderly. You must <u>never</u> <u>never</u> <u>never</u> remain seated when you're in the presence of an older person who is standing."

Should I stand up right now? In glancing around to see if anyone was wide awake enough to take her at her word, my eyes collided with Mitzi's -- laughing, secretive, friendly. It was a heady moment, that mutual, startled recognition of my own hidden potential for sass.

One day Mrs. Chumley brought scissors and colored paper. "Little Pitchers, why do I ask you to make bookmarks? So you will have no excuse to turn down the corners of a book's pages to mark your place. Nor do the well-bred moisten a finger to turn a page. Martin, do you ever engage in that despicable practice?"

Feet shuffled, seats creaked, as the class came to attention. A new boy, from Texas, Martin had joined us in January, to my big relief. Until then, I'd been the one, new in September, everyone suspiciously kept circling from afar.

9

"No, ma'am. I don't reckon I do."

"You prevaricate. I have seen you do it. You too, Crawford, but not Roberta; she's a little lady with impeccable manners. Martin, we Oregonians eschew words like reckon and ma'am. Some people call them colloquialisms, but I call them slang.

"Little Pitchers, slang is rude and churlish. It is especially offensive to use it for bodily functions. Ladies and gentlemen never use it, or what you imprecisely call dirty words. Words are not dirty. The mouths that use such words are dirty. That is why mothers of my day washed out their children's mouths with soap. Refined people also scorn baby talk -- pee-pee or poo-poo, or number one or number two. If you must mention those processes at all, use the scientific terms. Benjamin, do you know what the proper scientific terms are?"

He didn't. Neither did Betsy or Virginia or Carl.

"Bring out your pencils, children. U-r-i-n-a-t-e. Urinate. And d-e-f-e-c-a-t-e. Defecate."

Martin raised his hand. "Which one's which, ma'am?"

I held my breath. How could she explain it without using dirty words or baby talk?

She was saved by the bell.

At the popcorn wagon, Mitzi, Daniel, and Martin stood three abreast in front of me. "Mrs. Chumley's a royal pain in the butt," said Daniel.

Betsy, next to me, turned red. "Can you imagine telling anyone you want a hanky for a present?" she asked loudly.

Fran, also blushing, pointed at the black car rolling by. "Look, everybody. There goes Queen Roberta with her royal maid."

"I'll bet a nickel that prissy prig Roberta asks for hankies at Christmas," grinned Mitzi. "C'mon, Martin. Daniel and I'll show you our secret hideout."

Class was almost over the next week when Mrs. Chumley said, "Never ask, 'Mother, can I help you with the dishes?' That surprises you, does it not? I reiterate, Little Pitchers: Never ask 'Can I help,' because with the word can you are asking if you have the innate ability to help, and only you know that. Ask

10

instead, 'Mother, may I help you with the dishes?' because you thereby ask for permission to help. Mitzi, do you understand the signficant distinction between the two words?"

"That's nuts. I don't need permission to wipe the dishes. My mother <u>makes</u> me help."

"You are a rude little girl, and you will come in after school to learn some manners. You too, Daniel -- I saw that face you just made. Peggy, why would it be improper for you to hold up your hand and ask, 'Mrs. Chumley, can I go to the bathroom?'"

I took a deep breath, stunned by the sudden possibilities. But would I? Could I?

"Peggy? Where are your ears? Did you hear me?"

It was now or never. I stood up, closed my eyes, took another deep breath, and plunged. "Because I don't need to urinate or defecate."

Not a gasp, not a titter, only an eternal silence.

Finally, "Why, Peggy Brandstrom. I do believe you are a very rude little girl. You will report to me after school for a lesson in manners."

I stopped off at the girls' bathroom to comb my hair before reporting to Mrs. Chumley. Please curl for a change, I told my hair, almost sick with admiration for Mitzi's perky reddish-brown mop. Well, at least look scared, I told my reflection, but it couldn't help grinning. For weeks I'd imagined Mitzi and Daniel staying after school with Mrs. Chumley every Monday -- clapping erasers, giggling behind her back, sassing her every word. Now it was my turn to clap, giggle, and sass right along with them.

Halfway down the the shadowy, echoing hall to Mrs. Chumley's room I started tiptoeing. I'd never stayed after school before, never walked the halls alone.... Heart pounding, I ran the last few steps, almost threw myself at the door. Locked. Locked? How could it be locked? The door rumbled like thunder when I tried to shake it open.

I tried again, every day. On my way home Friday, I spotted Mitzi alone a block ahead of me and ran to catch up.

"Wait up, Mitzi. Weren't we supposed to stay after school on Monday?" She stared blankly. "For Mrs. Chumley. For sassing her in class, remember?"

"Oh she just natters. She's a harmless old thing."

"You mean ... you mean you never stay after school?"

"Of course not."

"But then why -- What happens? Does she tell your mother?"

"Tattle? She doesn't know the meaning of the word. Silly old thing -- she's all potatoes and no meat." She grinned, poked me with her elbow. "For crying out loud, didn't you even know that?"

"Well, of course I --"

But Mitzi had already skipped off, leaving me to stew in the hot, sticky juices of my own terrible shame.

Now what could I do about Dorie's problem? Mother was a nurse, so I didn't think Dorie was seriously sick, but as big sister I had an important mission. "Peggy, it's your job to look after little Dorie," Mother said, often. "That means you must always keep your eyes open for snares, pitfalls, and stumbling blocks."

Proud she left my assignment vague -- trusting me to recognize snares, pitfalls, and stumbling blocks when I saw them -- I tried never to ask for specific help. If I needed to know something more, I launched what Jack Armstrong, all-American boy, called a Listening-Post Operation: I crept halfway down the stairs to eavesdrop after they turned off the ten o'clock news. They spoke more openly then than they did in front of us, and they often spoke of the same worry that was chewing at me.

A few nights after my disgrace, Dorie interrupted her nightly litany. "Pah, Doh's not okay. Doh's legs hurt."

Why was Daddy so often out of town when I needed a Listening-Post Operation?

The next day she didn't want to dance with us when Harriet put a record on their phonograph. Mrs. McKay asked, "Is something the matter, Dorie? You always love to dance."

Dorie looked at me, almost crying. "I think her legs hurt."

Mrs. McKay checked for bruises. "Those look like perfectly good legs to me," she said. "You know what the trouble might be? I'll bet it's just growing pains."

Growing pains! Back home, I raced for Webster's. It defined them as "neuralgic pains or cramps occurring during growth," and defined neuralgia as "of or pertaining to nerves."

I patted Webster's, hugged myself. Mother sometimes sniffed "Just nerves!" when someone complained of a headache.

"Just nerves!" I told Dorie that night in bed. "Growing pains are a very good sign. It means you're stretching deep down inside -- like when you yawn. If you can put up with them for a while, one fine day you'll be just as big as I am."

"Doh's okay now, Pah. Doh has good growing pains," she murmured most nights. "Doh knows how to stretch inside." Better yet, every single thump of music sent her spinning into a dance.

But then came that afternoon in April....

It was the kind of spring day when the sun fights with one light rain after another, trying to come out. We were playing school in the kitchen nook. Mother, starting dinner, peppily sang "Yes, We Have No Bananas," but Dorie didn't stir from the table. Laziness, I hoped, watching her spell out words.

Herbie showed up at the window, wide open to the day. "Can Dorie come out and play?"

"Do you want to Dorie?" I asked when she didn't answer.

"No. Doh's tired."

"Sorry, Herbie. She doesn't want to."

"Aw please Dorie. The sun's out."

Dorie frowned, shook her head.

"No, Herbie. Go find Sonny. Dorie might have growing pains at the moment." She looked up to nod and smile.

"Sonny's not home. C'mon, Dorie."

"No, Herbie. I'm sorry, but we really do mean it. Dorie's too busy growing right now to take time out for playing."

"Yeah but --"

"Herbie! The answer is no. NO NO NO. Dorie needs to be left alone to grow for a while, because as you can see she has a lot of catching up to do."

Herbie finally left, grumbling, but a few minutes later my neck prickled; the dead silence in the kitchen warned me of trouble. I looked up to find Mother glaring from the archway, her hands on her hips in curled fists.

"What did I just hear you say, miss big mouth?"

I stared. I often sent Herbie away; it was one of my jobs to send him off nicely when he showed up when we were busy.

"Do you often talk about Dorie like that to your friends?"

Like how? "I was just --"

"You were just being too big for your britches, that's what you were being. Now get over here fast."

I knew what was coming but for the first time in my life I didn't know why. Too shocked to argue, I moved over, leaned down. Whatever my sin, it was a big one; three slaps on a bare bottom was the top penalty.

"Now you go upstairs and think about what you've said until dinner. And don't you ever let me hear you again making fun of your little sister."

She gave me another brisk slap as I went, then slapped the table for good measure.

And so for the very first time in my life, I didn't bawl like a baby when Mother spanked me. It did help -- it felt rather good to be unjustly punished for once -- but it didn't help very much. Dorie's heartbroken howls of sisterly sympathy followed me up the stairs, into our bedroom, and all the way into my dry but hotly steaming pillow.

II.
LITTLE LIES

We had enjoyed weeks of excitement by the time we moved from the Montavilla rental into the Couch Street house -- on a rainy June day when I was newly eight, Dorie almost six. Dorie and I raced from room to room, slithering in stocking feet on the slick hardwood floors. Mother followed behind, whispering, "It's a mansion, isn't it? It's a mansion, and it's <u>ours</u>."

She and Daddy had been inside before, but it was all new to us: an entry hall big enough for a baby grand piano ("Oh, Axel, maybe we'll get one someday?"); a dining room topped by a glittering chandelier; a green-and-cream kitchen with a sunny breakfast nook offside; two fireplaces -- one in the front room and one in the cozy adjoining room Daddy called "my den"; hide-and-seek closets in all three bedrooms; an upstairs bathroom bigger than our old kitchen. There was even a small room upstairs that Mother called "my sewing room."

"Some sewing room," I said, comparing it to Mother Barbour's retreat in "One Man's Family." "It doesn't have a window seat, or a fireplace, or a view of the sea wall, or room for --"

"Anna! Girls! Come, I've got a surprise." We found Daddy in his den. "Guess what's behind this door?"

"Another closet," said Mother.

"A surprise," said Dorie.

"A secret passage," said I. Thrilled, we all peered into the tiny half-bath they hadn't known was there.

"Oh, Axel, we've bought a blessed home."

It was a colonial, white with green shutters, two short blocks from Laurelhurst Park. And the park -- oh! the park: a four-by-six-block grassy, woodsy wonderland, criss-crossed by meandering paths, studded with wooden tables for picnicking families and benches for readers, knitters, dozers. On the large pond near Thirty-ninth, ducks and geese and swans squawked and flapped and dived for scraps. That wasn't all: On the far side of the main park, a block-square playground teemed with familiar playmates.

We'd been spending Sundays in the park all year, driving past 3511 all spring, and now we could see the tops of the park trees from our streetside windows. In those settling-in weeks Mother admired the park trees often, but found no time to take us there.

"Can't Dorie and I walk over alone?" I begged daily.

The snag was busy Burnside. Even after she showed us a route via the four-way stop at Thirty-ninth, Mother seldom let us go alone. She didn't insist on a grown-up; other children would do. But Harriet spent July at Seaside with her family; Alice always wanted to play house, or with dolls; and Cora Jean Rossi, from the next block, was usually busy with her best friend.

"So what's the use of living near a park?" I fretted all summer, annoyed that she <u>did</u> find time to lead us on practice walks to Laurelhurst School, nine blocks and two busy streets away.

"Mrs. McKay says there'll be safety officers here," she said, walking us across Thirty-ninth and then, a jog away, Glisan. "Do you promise to be careful? Or do I have to go with you?"

"I'm big enough to walk alone," I said, indignant.

"Me too," said Dorie, squeezing my hand.

As it turned out, only I went, and I went in a parade; half the front doors in our block opened simultaneously at a quarter past eight. Our ranks swelled with every block -- like Hamelin, I thought, pretending to pipe.

Though Harriet, Alice, and I started out three abreast, at first I walked the last blocks alone. They were a grade behind me, a distinction that counted within shadow of school. After school I stayed sociably with my class, but only Mitzi, Daniel, and Roberta lived beyond the Circle at Thirty-ninth and Glisan -- a tiny round park centered by a Joan of Arc statue and a streetcar shelter. Mitzi and Daniel followed their own secret route, and Roberta traveled grandly by car. Not that it mattered; from the Circle onward neighborhood loyalties took over.

"No one but me comes home for lunch," I complained regularly, with a bit of truth: No one beyond the Circle came home daily.

"The walk clears your brain," said Mother, unmoved.

I complained only on cold days. In open-window weather I could listen to "Pretty Kitty Kelly," uninterrupted, from one house to the next. It ran from eleven-thirty to noon; the minute Dorie shouted her welcome from the porch, Mother snapped it off, then turned on "Ma Perkins" at the stroke of twelve. So what was going on with Kitty that she didn't want me to hear?

I listened closely, almost fruitlessly.

"What does out of wet log mean?" I asked Harriet. "It has something to do with a baby that's on the way."

I didn't expect her to know, but her parents were less secretive than mine. When she grumbled "Don't your parents tell you <u>anything</u>?" she was only pretending; she was always pleased when I trusted her with a secret fact-gathering mission.

She brought back an answer the next day. "It's wet lock, not wet log. Unfortunate babies are sometimes born out of wet lock, and that makes them illegitimate."

"Illegitimate? What does that mean?"

"I just told you. Out of wet lock."

"But I still don't know what...." How could I break her dead-end circle?

Her chin went out. "Well, that's all you need to know."

I'd learned to he careful when her chin was out. "Please, Harriet, something's missing. Could you ask her again? For -- for familiar words?"

She came over later to say it was wedlock, not wet lock. "Out of wedlock means not married -- no wedding. Unfortunate babies are sometimes born out of wedlock, and that means their parents aren't married, and that means the babies are illegitimate."

"Pooh. People <u>have</u> to be married to have babies.

"My mother says they don't."

"My mother says they do." Oh-oh. Could that be a lie? Had she really said so, or just let me think so?

17

"Are you calling my mother a liar?" Her chin was out a foot.

"Of course not. Parents don't lie. But how can --"

"I won't answer questions if you don't believe what I say."

I didn't, and she wouldn't, so she went home in a huff.

At Christmas the huge Webster's arrived. The first time Dorie and I were home alone, I ran to it, flipped through the pages to <u>illegitimate</u>. The first definition -- "unlawfully begotten; born out of wedlock; bastard" -- sent me to the <u>b</u>'s. No trace of <u>begotten</u>; under <u>bastard</u> I found: "a 'natural' child; a child begotten and born out of wedlock; one born of an illicit union."

<u>Illicit</u> came through with "not permitted or allowed; improper, unlawful, as illicit trade, intercourse." Heartened -- at home with the concept of not allowed -- I looked up <u>intercourse</u>: "sexual connection, as illicit intercourse."

Blinking, I turned back to <u>illegitimate</u>: "Not legitimately deduced; illogical, as illegitimate inference ... unlawful . . . not authorized by good usage, as an illegitimate word ... out of the ordinary, unusual, abnormal." This seemed to be the wrong path, so I turned back to <u>bastard</u> and was heading for <u>sexual</u> when our car came up the driveway. I slammed the dictionary shut, re-considered, then opened it to the innocent <u>m</u>'s and put Daddy's magnifying glass on top.

"I've had an illegitimate lesson," I told Dorie, practicing the syllables and their flow. "An illicit one, too." Neither sat very easily on my tongue; it would take practice.

Helping unload groceries, teasing myself, I sang "It's a long way through dictionaries, It's a long way to go...." I still didn't quite know what Kitty Kelly was up to, but I knew the answer was waiting for me somewhere in that great big wonderful (chinless!) Webster's, if only I could find my way.

From the first days at Laurelhurst, I was one of the three best spellers in my class. Every Monday morning Mrs. Adams gave us thirty words to study for our Friday afternoon spelling bee. If we weren't captains (winner and runner-up of the last one), Mary

Jane Farris, Betsy Baum, and I were always the first ones chosen as each team lined up on opposite sides of the room.

"Captain A, the first word is neighborhood," Mrs. Adams said, rapping on her desk for hushed attention.

Captain A moved forward one step. "Neighborhood. Nay-bore-hood. N-e-i-g-h, b-o-r, h-o-o-d. It's nice to live in a friendly neighborhood."

The ones who went to their seats early blushed in disappointment and shame; everyone wanted to last for the surprise words -- the new and tricky ones Mrs. Adams brought out when only four members on each team remained standing.

"Necessary," I said, eyes closed. "Ness-ess-air-ee. N-e-c, e-s, s-a-r, y. It isn't necessary to cheat in school."

Cheering or groaning? I couldn't open my eyes until I knew what my side was doing. Tears clogged my throat, ready for failure -- but ready for glory if I won for my side.

After Webster's moved in, we had spelling matches at home too, at our Sunday evening games, when we ate supper in the kitchen nook. ("Wholesome peasant food" Mother called it, but it was more like breakfast: things like nuts and raisins in rice in winter, bananas in cornflakes in summer.) All week long Daddy and I collected words for each other, then brought our lists to the table and handed them to Mother.

As teacher, she cut our lists to fifteen words each. Dorie was my backup squad; I wrote each word on a magic slate so she could spell it too. She was also cheerleader. Whenever one of us spelled a word correctly, she jumped up to clap, wiggle, and shout "Rah for Dah!" or "Three rahs for Doh and Pah!"

The night I gave Daddy the word illegitimate, Mother interrupted as soon as he'd spelled it. "Wait a minute, Axel. Let's hear Peggy use it in a sentence."

Ah ha, I thought. "It's illegitimate to -- to cross the street on a red light." Their smiles tempted me to push a bit. "It's like illegal. But how can a word be illegal?"

Daddy nodded. "Good question. America protects freedom of speech, doesn't it? It means that some words are inferior, or misused."

"Like swear words? Or like ain't and swell?"

19

Mother winked at Daddy; still, I knew better than to push them about illegitimate babies. When Mother said (often), "You go too far, child. Do you always have to <u>push</u> so hard?" she was just like Harriet when her chin stuck straight out -- unreachable and unsmiling for hours.

We played other word games too, some of them based on Daddy's box of ten booklets called <u>English for the Foreign-born</u>; they reminded me of my arithmetic workbook because each lesson had a test at the end, with spaces to fill in. So instead of pushing, I asked, "What's next week's game?"

"Well, let me think.... Do you know what the famous difference is between <u>which</u> and <u>that?</u>" I shook my head. "Okay, hand me your slate." He printed three sentences:

I'LL REMOVE THE BOWL THAT CONTAINS FOUR PEARS FROM THE TABLE.

I'LL REMOVE THE BOWL, WHICH CONTAINS FOUR PEARS, FROM THE TABLE.

I'LL REMOVE THE BOWL WHICH CONTAINS FOUR PEARS FROM THE TABLE.

"Now tell me what you would mean by the first sentence."

After a moment I pointed at a bowl on our table. "I'll remove <u>that</u> bowl."

"Good. The word <u>that</u> points at something specific, as you just did -- at the fruit bowl, not our rice bowls. Now look at the second sentence. Does it mean exactly the same thing?"

I frowned, wriggled, sighed. At last something came. "Why did you put in the commas?"

"You're getting warm. Keep thinking."

Again I steamed until something came. "Because the bowl just happens to have four pears in it?"

"You're getting there. Think some more. How many things do you tell me in the second sentence?"

"Well.... Two? I'm going to remove the bowl, and the bowl happens to have four pears in it." Light struck. "The commas are like brackets, aren't they? They're there to tuck something out of the way."

He grinned, reached over to pat my head; Dorie jumped up to clap and cheer with Mother; and I took bows, as proud as if I'd won a world championship.

"Good girl. The commas fence off an extra fact -- perhaps interesting but extra just the same. Even if you put your finger over the fenced-off words the sentence still works. Try it. What do you have left?"

"I'll remove the bowl from the table."

"Right. Now try it with the first sentence."

"Nothing's fenced off. There's nothing extra.

"Right. It's a one-fact sentence. So now tell me how many facts the third sentence contains."

"Just one -- nothing's fenced off. It's like the first one."

"Now you've got it. It says the same thing as the first one, but says it wrong. It's an illegitimate which -- and that's next week's game. We'll each collect five sentences with which and five with that from our reading, and test each other on the examples.... Let's make up five examples of each too. Okay?"

Mother stood up. "Let's take the bowl that contains four pears to the front room. It's time for Jack Benny."

Only on Sunday evenings did we walk away from the dishes.

If Sunday evening was my favorite time of the week, Sunday morning was Dorie's. All day Saturday she crooned "Tomorrow Doh and Pah go to Sunday school"; from time to time she slipped into our closet to pat our Sunday dresses; at bedtime she hung them on the door and spread our other clothes out on the dressers.

We kept going to our Montavilla Sunday school for over a year. "It takes time to find the right new one," Mother said, frowning, whenever I asked her why. Finally one fall day she announced that we'd start next Sunday at a new one. "Walking distance -- on Ankeny, behind the drugstore. Isn't that wonderful?"

It met at ten o'clock, an hour before church, in a basement room furnished with round tables, a desk, a portable blackboard, and a piano. The preschoolers sat at low tables at one end, but Miss Sarah let Dorie sit with me.

21

"I'm the new girl again," I complained afterwards to Mother. "I expected to know everybody."

She explained: It wasn't a neighborhood church; it was Presbyterian. The McKays were Presbyterian, but attended the main church downtown. Alice's family was Episcopalian; Cora Jean's, Catholic; Mitzi's and Daniel's, Jewish.

"Come to think of it, the Northrups are Presbyterian too -- Lucille McKay said something once about working on some church committee with Mrs. Northrup. It would be really good news to me if you made friends with Roberta."

I made a face she couldn't see; she'd been saying that ever since she met Roberta and her family one Parents' Night.

"We'll join because of you girls, but we're not Presbyterians either. My family is Baptist, Daddy's Lutheran. Except Grandpa, suddenly. He's born-again." She paused, looked at me. "Not that it matters. Does it?"

Not that what matters? "Sarah's the only one I know, but she's the teacher, and I'm supposed to call her Miss Sarah now."

"Well, that's a start, isn't it? You like her. And she's new, too. Today was her first time. You can be new together."

I nodded; I liked her a lot. She was Eleanor Holden's big sister, a student at business college. When she took care of us on the nights Mother and Daddy went to their season-ticket concerts, she brought Nancy Drew to read aloud -- a big step upward from the Bobbsey twins and Honeybunch.

In class the Sunday after Thanksgiving, my neck prickled; someone was staring at me. I felt creepier still when I looked up -- straight across the room into the blank gray eyes of Roberta. After a moment I smiled. She didn't. The little girl next to her waved.

"Hi, Noh!" said Dorie, jumping up to wave back, and I remembered seeing her at Herbie's birthday party. So Queen Roberta had a little sister?

"Shh Dorie. It's quiet time." I looked around for Miss Sarah, found her right behind me.

"It's all right, Peggy. But I see Dorie and Noreen are old friends. Maybe next week they'd like to sit together with the younger ones."

22

As we arrived the next Sunday, Roberta waved at us. "Noreen's saving a seat for your sister, and I've saved this one for you."

"Okay, Dorie? Do you want to sit with Noreen?"

"Hi, Noh. Bye-bye Pah," she said, trotting off.

After that, Roberta hardly opened her mouth, or even looked my way -- Dorie and Noreen whispered together more than we did. So why did she bother saving me a seat every Sunday? And who wanted to be friends with prissy old Roberta anyway?

Then one Sunday, as we were filing up the stairs at the end of class, she grabbed my arm.

"Are your parents coming to church today?"

"Maybe. Why?"

"To ask them if you can play at our house until after church."

Wow. "Maybe," I said, and headed out to the front of the church to find them.

"Of course," said Mother. "Just remember dinner's at two."

"Good," said Roberta. "Let's go to the play park."

I wasn't allowed, without asking first. But we were now technically under the Northrup's care, already safely across Burnside .... "You bet. Are your parents in church too?"

"Not here. Downtown. They won't be home until about one."

"How come you're going to this Sunday school now?"

"My father finally put his foot down." She stopped in her tracks, looked at me big-eyed. "You should've heard him. 'SWEET JUMPING JESUS!' he screamed. 'It's crazy to wait around downtown for an hour.' Mother said Sophie could deliver us, but he said we could damn well walk a block and a half to this one."

"Who's Sophie?"

"Our maid."

We started walking again. "You're really lucky, living right across the street from the park. Do you go every day?"

"No. Dorie won't tattle, will she?"

"Dorie never tattles."

Roberta laughed. I'd never even seen her smile before. Her mouth was full of metal. "I wish I had braces," I said, surprised to hear it. She snapped her mouth shut.

"I damn well mean it."

"Sweet jumping Jesus," she said, laughing again.

The play park was almost empty in the gray December cold. We tumbled from the swings to the teeter-totters to the slides to the rings. The little girls shrieked happily as they skidded over the icy, not-quite-empty wading pool. I started to shush them, but who was close enough to hear?

I jumped when Roberta gripped my arm. "Peggy, see that man by the sandbox? He's a kidnapper, on the lookout for a victim."

"He is not. He's not even a man. He's Betsy Baum's big brother Mose."

"Well, he's up to something shady. I bet he's a dope fiend. Why does he keep staring at us?"

He wasn't just staring; he was coming our way.

"Maybe he wants to ply us with demon rum," I whispered, grabbing Dorie's hand. She grabbed Noreen's, who grabbed Roberta's; we all edged towards the swings, in sight of street traffic.

"He probably wants to ravage us. That's what kikes do to little girls, you know."

"What's a --"

Another boy -- bigger still, with wild red hair -- came loping like a gorilla from the corner behind us ... and our parents didn't know where we were.

"We're being surrounded -- run for your lives!"

Hand in hand, a waving human chain, we ran for Thirty-ninth, bang into a third high-school boy who was walking a bike.

"Hey girls," he said, making a little lunge at us. "Hey Mose. Hey Bobbo."

We ran all the way to Ankeny. "A very narrow escape," said Roberta, smiling a glittering smile. She slowed down, headed us across the street towards her house.

"We made it by the skin of our teeth," I agreed gratefully. "You're a born leader. A born-again leader."

From the inside, her house wasn't unfriendly at all, though we didn't get very far into it. We piled our coats on a chair and had barely settled on the hall rug with pickup-sticks when her parents bustled in. I scrambled to my feet.

"I hear that you're the best speller in Roberta's class," said Mrs. Northrup.

Oh-oh: Muddy water squished from my shoes.

"What does your father do, Peggy?" Mr. Northrup asked.

"Do? Daddy?"

"What business is he in?"

"Business? I don't think --"

"Doesn't he go to an office?"

"Oh yes. Sometimes." Then I remembered. "Mostly he goes out into the field. He's a logger. An old Swedish logger."

"Is that so. Well."

"He's a lumberjack. Like Paul Bunyan."

Mrs. Northrup rang a little bell. A gray-haired woman came to take their coats. "How soon is dinner, Sophie? Take Roberta's shoes too, please, and Noreen's. Have you girls been sitting here in wet shoes ever since Sunday school?"

"Yes, I'm afraid so," said Roberta, looking her mother straight in the eye.

"Doesn't Sophie ever tattle about our park visits?" I asked a few Sundays later. In real school we never spoke; our Sunday friendship was secret. I didn't know why, nor did I mind. I did mind that Mother wanted us to take turns on which house we went to after Sunday school; I was running out of excuses.

"Sophie? She's just a maid. Why would she tattle?"

Whatever the McKays' Jane or the Doles' Mrs. Schultz overheard got to our parents fast. "Isn't it her job to tell?"

"Sophie's a maid, and knows her place."

"Doesn't she mind being called a maid?" Mrs. McKay had told us, firmly, to call Jane their girl, or their live-in; she was a college girl who helped out in exchange for room and board, and "She deserves your respect." Alice had ordered us to call Mrs.

25

Schultz a housekeeper; she wasn't just a cleaning lady because she came every weekday and left dinner in the oven. "Why don't you call her your girl, or your housekeeper?"

"She's too old to be called a girl. Why should she mind being called a maid? That's what she is. And she lives in the maid's room, or hadn't you noticed?"

"I don't know. It doesn't sound nice. In our block --"

"What do you know about it? Your mother doesn't even have help, does she?"

Humbled, I shook my head, wondering why not and how Roberta knew. Not totally humbled: "Well, I think she's too old to be called either a maid or Sophie. What's her last name?"

"How should I know? Her family lives down by the river."

What did the river have to do with it? I didn't bother asking, but resolved to ask Mrs. Northrup for Sophie's last name the next time I stood tongue-tied before her. I'd look her straight in the eye, smile pleasantly, and.... She'd be lots less scary in an apron and flat shoes, like other mothers.

A week or two later, for the first time, we got back from the park in time to collect milk from the kitchen and head upstairs to Roberta's room. Dozens of dolls stood primly on shelves; lacy cushions sat plumply on a window seat; a canopied single bed stood alone in an alcove.

"Doesn't Noreen sleep here too?"

"Of course not. Dorie, don't sit on the bed -- it's not for sitting on. And don't touch those dolls -- they're not for playing with. SWEET JUMPING JESUS! Doesn't she know anything?"

Startled, Dorie backed into Roberta, knocking the milk tray to the floor. As I dived for the rolling glasses, Roberta darted to the door. "SOPHIE! Bring a mop -- fast!" She stomped her foot, slapped herself on the forehead, made a face. "How can you stand living with it?"

With what? Dorie's lower lip was out and trembling. "It's okay, Dorie. It wasn't your fault."

"Oh yeah? Then whose fault was it?"

"Yours. You scared her when you yelled. You scared me too, but I wasn't standing right in front of you."

26

Voices from downstairs told me the Northrups were home. I dumped the glasses on the tray. "We have to go now."

We met Sophie on the stairs, but the entry hall was empty. We'd almost reached the coat closet when Mrs. Northrup called from the front room.

"Girls? Why are you being so quiet? Come in for a moment."

She looked up from the Sunday paper. "Did you girls enjoy the morning?" I nodded, mute and sweaty. "Roberta, what was the fuss with Sophie?"

"I don't want to tattle."

"Telling the truth is never tattling."

"Dorie knocked over our milk. All four glasses."

Where was my tongue? It was Roberta, not Dorie, who'd dropped the tray. And it was Roberta who -- "Oh, well.... We don't cry over spilled milk, do we?"

"Poor little thing. It really scared her."

Both smiled at Dorie; she smiled back. "Doh didn't mean to."

"I'm sure you didn't, Dorie.... Peggy, would you tell your Mother that I'd like to call on her Tuesday afternoon? At about two o'clock. She can call me if it isn't convenient."

I nodded again. Could we go now? But I felt stuck on the end of her stare, like a fish on a spear, until suddenly she laughed.

"By the way, Peggy, you shouldn't go around telling people that your father's a lumberjack."

"I shouldn't? Why not?"

"He isn't, you know. You're telling a lie."

"But that's what --"

"He's a forest economist. He's the senior forest economist of the Pacific Northwest. That's a far cry from Paul Bunyan, my little dear."

We tore home. The race cleared our brains.

"Doh wins. Doh beats Pah again," Dorie laughed not even panting. (She always won. "Doh knows how to be the wind," she'd explained, but it didn't work for me.)

"Rah rah for you, Dorie. Now if you go wash your face, we won't have to tell Mother about the milk."

She skipped off. I pounded into the kitchen. "Mother, what does Daddy do?"

"Do? When?" She was concentrating on the gravy.

"What business is he in?"

"He's a forester, of course. For the U.S. Forest Service. And he writes textbooks about selective logging. Douglas firs. You know that."

I stomped my foot. "You never told me."

"Don't be silly. You've known that for years. That's why we finally bought this house -- to celebrate his appointment. It was a hard decision for him to make. He loved teaching."

"Teaching?"

"Maybe you don't remember that. Before we moved to Portland he taught at the University of Washington."

"But he always says he's an old Swedish logger, making his way in the new world."

She looked up, smiling. "Yes. He does like to say that."

"But that's a lie. He's been lying to me."

"For Pete's sake, child. That's not a lie. That's a joke. Daddy likes to be funny."

At dinner she asked, "Peggy, who asked about Daddy's work?"

"Mrs. Northrup. She wants to call on you on Tuesday. In the afternoon -- around two o'clock."

"Does she? That's nice. I've been thinking about calling on her, now that you and Roberta are becoming such good friends."

Oh no we weren't, I decided, flooded with the relief of discovering a clear path ahead. I put my fork down. "We went to the play park this morning."

"Without telling us first? You know better than that."

"We went last week too."

She stared at me. "Does their housekeeper take you?"

"No. We go alone. Just the four of us."

"And you didn't tell us? I don't like that kind of carelessness. Surely Roberta isn't that careless with her parents?"

It wasn't quite a question, so I kept pushing. "We've been going every Sunday. For weeks and weeks."

"And kept it a secret from us?" She shook her head, looked over at Daddy.

"Peggy, you're the big sister, and you're in charge," said Daddy. "You know we need to trust you, don't you?"

"I'm sorry," I said, sorrier than they knew; Mother turned things over to Daddy only when she'd had her say.

"Well, better late than never," she said. "I'm glad you're telling us now. I just knew that Roberta would be a good example for you."

"Roberta's really sassy sometimes. You should hear how she talks to their housekeeper."

"Nonsense. She's a wonderful influence on you. That's what good friends do -- bring out the best in each other. Do you understand that?"

"She's too sassy for her own good," I muttered as I nodded, defeated, because I also understood something that wasn't fair at all: By Mother's lights, Roberta could do no wrong, just as Mitzi could do no right.

But I didn't understand, later -- at the dictionary, where I found eight paragraphs defining <u>forester</u>, two lines under <u>logger</u>, and only one word for <u>lumberjack</u> -- why two tiny, tidy, uninvited tears sneaked out of my eyes to slip noiselessly down my cheeks.

III.
AIDING AND ABETTING

"No," I told Harriet the next afternoon when she wanted me to come out and play. "I'm skewered on the horns of a dilemma."

She blinked, frowned, formed a worried "Oh" with her lips, then backed down the front porch steps, awed. She too had heard Daddy Warbucks discuss those portentous words with Annie.

What could I do? "Skewered," I discovered, wasn't the right word at all for a dilemma. I went around and around, back and forth, jumping from one sticky horn to the other.

Now that I'd tattled on myself, I was honor bound to warn Roberta about what her mother might uncover on her Tuesday visit. But how could I break the rules of a pact so secret I didn't know when or why we'd made it? Nor did I want to break them, much; if I warned her, she'd think I really liked her....

Worse: If Mother discovered Mrs. Northrup knew nothing of our park visits, she'd know I'd cooperated, through silence, in the deception -- a spanking for sure, even if I confessed ahead of time. A spanking I could live through, but she liked Roberta too much to blame her at all, so she'd be more convinced than ever that I needed Roberta's friendship as a good example.

Unless.... If I didn't warn Roberta, would I get rid of her nicely? Could I trust her to hate me for betraying her?

No. I probably couldn't. She might just get meaner, bossier, sneakier, crankier. So maybe I should head that off by....

Despite my prayers, Tuesday morning arrived. So did Tuesday afternoon, bringing the dreaded, dreadful moment, after school, when there was no place to go but up the driveway and into the jaws of punishment.

Dorie wasn't waiting at the door -- a very bad omen. Mother sat in the living room, working on needlepoint, cups still on the coffee table -- another bad omen.

"Where's Dorie?" If I could just dash through, innocently heading for the den closet, maybe....

"Sit down, Peggy. I want to talk to you."

Here it comes. I sank into the couch.

"You just missed Jessamyn Northrup."

Did the hall clock always tick so noisily?

"She invited you to a luncheon downtown. A week from Saturday. Roberta's tenth birthday." She snipped a thread, looked up with a big smile. "Roberta was almost a Valentine baby."

"Lunch?" Birthday parties were always cake and ice cream.

"She's reserved a table for six at the Orange Lantern."

"For six?" Birthday parties were for the whole block, or the whole class. "Dorie too?"

"No."

"Harriet? Alice?"

"No. Or I don't suppose so. They're not special friends like you, are they?"

"Then who else? Anyone from our class?"

She shrugged. "I didn't ask who else was invited."

I had never before been invited to a lunch party in a restaurant. Luncheon. I licked my lips, stared at the pattern on the Oriental carpet. Why couldn't Roberta ever do things the way everyone else did?

"Aren't you pleased? Seems to me that's pretty exciting."

I had never been away alone on Saturday. "Dorie loves birthday parties. She'd hurt, maybe, if she couldn't go too."

Mother sighed. "Yes. Yes, I suppose so." She stared at me, sighed again. "Peggy, don't you want to go?"

I nodded, aching with both relief and longing. My voice came out in a whisper. "Could we tell Dorie I'm going to the dentist or something? I know it's a lie, but --"

"I know, child. Let me talk it over with Daddy."

On Saturday morning we went downtown. Mother usually made our clothes, so she was as excited as we were by the endless racks of girls' dresses. We found Dorie's first: a swirly-skirted taffeta one in shimmering cherry pink.

32

"She's so petite she's cute in anything," said the saleslady. "But let's try a chubbette for your older girl."

She carried off the rejects, brought in others. I fell for a princess-style velveteen in bright royal blue. Mother liked a flowered silk one better, but agreed that the velveteen one was more slenderizing, better with my pale Swedish coloring.

"Now for Roberta's present," said Mother. "Any ideas?"

"She collects dolls, but not regular ones. They're small and skinny, in long skirts. Aprons ... scarves ...."

"National costumes, I suppose. You buy them in foreign lands, or through catalogs. Well, let's try the book department."

"A big-little book, that's what she'd like," I said in the elevator. "A big-little book," I said again as we moved from one table to the next. "We can get it at the dime store."

Mother wanted to give her <u>Heidi</u>, or <u>Swiss Family Robinson</u>.

"No," I said. "We read those in school."

"How about Greek myths?"

"No no no," I said, getting cranky. Whose friend was she anyway? "A big-little book."

"We are <u>not</u> giving her one of those cheap little books." Suddenly as cranky as I was, Mother herded us over to Penney's for stockings to match our new dresses.

"Can I have barrettes too? Like Roberta's -- but royal blue."

"Where would you put them?"

Dorie and I had Dutch-boy bobs, square in front and shingled in back. Roberta wore hers longer, to her collar; it swooped back from a central part into barrettes that, like her hair, were the color of milk chocolate.

"I'm letting my bangs grow out. Maybe they'll grow fast."

They didn't, but we both felt very smart, on Friday after school, as we strutted around the front room in our new finery, jauntily topped with Mother's surprise: Scotch glengarries, made from the leftover fabric of our matching gray winter coats.

"Little ladies wear gloves, too," she said, showing us how to smooth them over our fingers in a ladylike manner.

Harriet showed up in time to admire us. "Oooh, hats and gloves -- you remind me of the March girls," she said. "Let's play little women."

Dorie was Beth ("I'll teach you how to die tragically," said Harriet, insisting that Dorie take off her coat, hat, and gloves to do so); Harriet was Amy; I was Jo; Meg was out calling. When Daddy came home we treated him to a fancy-dress parade, with Harriet prancing in front like a drum majorette.

"What about my present for Roberta?" I remembered at dinner.

"Oh, I found the dearest handkerchief box at Meier and Frank's Friday surprise sale. Lace and petit point, with shepherdesses in lavender dresses to match the lavender sachet."

"A handkerchief box?"

"And when you lift the lid it plays the Brahms lullaby. You'll just love it, Peggy. You can wrap it after dinner."

I was still stubborn, brave Jo when I refused even to look at it. Later, after our baths, I was only a poor little match girl.

"Please, Mother, I can't give her a handkerchief box. She'll hate it, I know. That's not a kid's gift. I won't go if --"

She put a finger on my lips. "Hush, child. She'll love it, I promise you."

From the curb, waiting for the Northrups, I waved at Dorie, framed in the picture window in her new party dress. All morning she'd murmured, "Today Pah goes to lunch with Rahtah. Doh goes to lunch with Mah and Dah." They were going to Jolly Joan's.

Without me.

No one spoke as I loaded into the back seat. "Happy birthday, Roberta," I said, my heart sinking as I handed her my present; at Sunday school I'd give her some of my big-little books. Noreen took my package from her, dropped it into the basket on her lap.

A little white-haired lady sat between the Northrups. "Peggy, this is our dear Aunt Martha," said Mrs. Northrup. She didn't turn around; neither did Aunt Martha. Should I call her that? And were we the six? Just their family and me?

Mr. Northrup dropped us on a Broadway corner, went to park the car. A creaky elevator in an office building took us up to the Orange Lantern.

"We're early," said Mrs. Northrup. "Noreen and I will see to the table. You can wait here in the foyer for the others."

So this was a foyer -- like a dentist's waiting room, with straight chairs along the sides and a coat tree in a corner. Roberta was unbuttoning her coat -- navy blue with a velveteen collar; she wore a velveteen beret and navy blue stockings.

"My stockings match my dress." I opened my coat to show her.

"So do mine." She took off her coat and hung it up. Her dress was navy wool -- a color and fabric I'd refused to consider. "Bright colors can be so vulgar, don't you think?"

Was she saying something mean? I took off my coat anyway. "Aren't you going to take your hat off?"

"Ladies don't take their hats off in public places."

But mine didn't match my dress. Flushing, I stuffed it into my coat pocket. Mitzi was right. Roberta was a prig.

"What a pretty dress, Patty," said Aunt Martha, so loud that I jumped.

"Thank you. I'm glad --"

"Don't bother," said Roberta. "Know any dirty words?" I stared blankly. "She's deaf as a post." She touched Aunt Martha's knee, smiled into her face. "DAMN IT TO BLAZING SMITHEREENS."

Aunt Martha smiled back. "Your dress is pretty too."

"Now it's your turn."

"H-E-double-toothpicks." When Roberta shook her head, I got braver. "To hell on a high horse."

"No, no, no. You've got to smile as you say it. And yell. TO HELL ON A HORSE, AUNTIE. AND GO SPIT IN THE STINKING SINK."

Phooey and double phooey? Out of wedlock? The door flew open -- to Roberta's father, leading four girls in navy blue coats.

"Hail, hail, the gang's all here," he sang. "Look who I found in the elevator, looking for a birthday party."

35

"Whom," said Mrs. Northrup, coming in from the restaurant. "Welcome, girls. You've found your party."

Roberta introduced us. Catherine and Carolyn -- twins -- were the daughters of Mr. Northrup's "medical colleague." Pauline was Roberta's cousin. "And this is Bean. Her mother is my mother's best friend, so Bean and I've been best friends all our lives."

Did mothers have best friends? I wondered, saying "How do you do" nicely, four times in a row.

"And Peggy's my new friend -- from school and Sunday school both. She lives two short blocks away from us."

Didn't any of them know how to smile? Or how to say "How do you do" back? But I hated Bean less when I saw her bright red dress, less still when she stuffed her hat into her pocket. And all hate dissolved when I saw our table: round, with a pink tablecloth, centered with a bouquet of baby roses and ten flickering candles as slender and long as brand new pencils. At each place a pink napkin, folded like a fan, stood guard; on each plate, a long-stemmed rose topped a tiny pink package.

"Now you young ladies enjoy yourselves," said Mrs. Northrup. "We'll be out here at another table if you need us for anything."

Two waitresses swished a leafy curtain around us, magically enclosing us in the hush of our own shadowy, shimmering, rose-scented bower. Blinking, breathing deep, I wondered if I would ever be the same old ordinary Brandstrom girl again....

It was after five o'clock when I got home. Still in her new dress, Dorie sat on the hall rug, playing jacks with Herbie. Daddy, working at the dictionary in the den, grunted as I hung up my coat. Mother was browning pork chops for dinner.

"Here comes the party girl," she said, clapping. "Was it wonderful?"

"It was okay." I handed her my rose, now hanging its head.

"Only okay? I can't believe that. Wasn't it fun?"

I shrugged, feeling all those cold eyes on me when Roberta announced that everyone's father but mine was "an eminent local physician." ("Well, mine's an eminent local forester," I'd said. "In fact, he was born in Sweden, so he's an eminent worldwide forester." They'd stared then too, until Roberta's eyes finally sparkled, crinkled into a smile. "By gosh, that's true.")

"Why didn't you tell me Roberta's father was an eminent local physician?"

"I forgot, I suppose. Who else was there?"

"Aunt Martha's deaf as a post." I couldn't help laughing, remembering. "She's Mr. Northrup's -- Dr. Northrup's -- aunt. As old as Grandpa but lots nicer."

"No other girls?"

"Four girls from the Heights. We had our own little room, with a cloth wall. The family ate in the main dining room."

"What did you eat?"

"Oh, Mother, the cutest little chicken pies. A whole one each. But first we had soup, then salad. Roberta said her family has four-course meals all the time. Why don't we?"

"I guess I never thought of it."

"And she gave us each a present. A little envelope of bath salts, with her name and birth date printed on it. For our memory books, she said, long after the bath salts are gone."

"Oh my -- presents for the guests. That's real class. Why were you so late?"

She was curious, not mad. "The rest of us stayed downtown while Roberta's father drove the girls home. All four girls live on the same block in Arlington Heights, and he went in to visit with his brother -- Pauline's father. He smelled just like Christmas glugg when he picked us up."

"You must be mistaken, miss smart aleck. I hope you didn't say that."

"Of course not." But Roberta had, secretly; she'd rolled her eyes, thrown her head back, and pretended to swig from a glass.

"Tell me about the other girls."

"They were okay, I guess." I wasn't ready to talk about them. Like Roberta, the twins and Pauline had straight hair, medium length and medium brown; all were as lean, graceful, and colorless as greyhounds. Bean was stubby, with orange freckles and pigtails. She and Roberta whispered together all through lunch, so why did I like her best? Better than Roberta, even?

"You should have told me that ladies don't take off their hats in public places. And my hat should match my dress, for when I take off my coat."

"My oh my, miss snippy -- you are in a proper mood. Maybe you're not big enough for fancy luncheons. Was something wrong with your hat?"

"No, I love it," I admitted, remembering how grown up I'd felt running around the shops alone with Roberta. (Dr. Northrup had given us each a dime, and asked how we spent them as soon as we got into the car. "Double chocolate ice cream cones," said Roberta, elbowing me. "Mine was strawberry," I'd said, elbowing back.) "I love my whole outfit."

Mother checked the clock. "Well, I'm afraid the ball is over. Send Herbie home, and get out of your party dresses for dinner."

I was glad to go. For one thing, I didn't want Mother to notice the condition of my shoes. For another -- "By the way, did Roberta like her handkerchief box?"

"I guess so," I said, skedaddling.

I had a lot of thinking to do, but I saved it until we were in bed with our light out.

First: Why did Roberta lie about how we'd spent our dimes? I didn't mind cooperating on harmless fibs, but why did she want to hide our shoeshines? Throned on high outside the Heathman Hotel, I'd felt like King Arthur, watching commoners scurry by at our feet. Why waste a lie on something as innocent -- as admirable, even -- as getting clean, shining shoes?

Second: Why on earth had she been so excited over my handkerchief box? She liked it better than Pauline's diary, the twins' dolls, Bean's subscription to Playmate. "Ooooh, Peggy" she'd breathed, her eyes flashing. "I love it. How did you know?"

The big question: How had Mother known? And why did it seem such a very bad omen that she had? And why hadn't -- "Pah and Doh sing?" asked Dorie.

"Sure," I said, meeting her hand. "You choose."

38

At least, I thought, slipping off to Yankee Doodle, my dilemma had disappeared into the mist like Cinderella's coach ... and puzzlements weren't nearly as heavy or sticky as dilemmas.

"When's your birthday?" Roberta asked after Sunday school.

"Next month. March eighteenth." Did she hope I might give a party like hers? "Why?"

"Ask for a bicycle. That's what my parents gave me, but I can't go out on it alone. Think of the fun we'd have."

Mother's unshakable arguments against a bike were that neither Harriet nor Alice had one yet; Cora Jean had one, but she was a whole year older; and Mitzi had one, but she was a bad example – "Reason enough, miss, for you not to get any big ideas."

"Oh wow. Can we go see it?"

We sneaked into her garage, whispering even though the car was gone. A black and silver Schwinn, it still wore birthday ribbons.

"Oh my. Balloon tires."

Roberta circled the garage, wheels wobbling. "Want to try?"

I shook my head. "I'll get my own."

We were already at the play park when I remembered to ask why she'd kept our shoeshines a secret.

"Maybe I just like secrets."

"That's no answer."

She squatted down to tie her shoes. "If you get a bike --"

"Please, Roberta! I can't help you lie unless I know why we're lying. What do your parents have against shoeshines?"

"Nothing, but.... Can you keep a secret?"

I answered by stomping my foot. Hadn't she even noticed what a good secret-keeper I'd been?

"Noreen, why don't you and Dorie race to the swings? Peggy and I will time you from the bench over there."

We settled down. "I think he's a peon," she whispered.

Had she changed the subject? "Who?"

"Pedro. The shoeshine man."

"Him? He's only a boy. High school, I'd say."

"Well, whatever. I think he's a peon."

39

"What's a peon?"

"Oh, you know. Like a kike. Or a Chink."

"What's a kike?"

"A yid. A Jew. Daniel's a kike, and Benny. So are Mitzi and Betsy. Doesn't your mother ever tell you anything?"

"Of course she does. She told me months ago who's Jewish and who's Catholic and who's -- but so what?"

Roberta looked shocked. "We mustn't have any truck with them. We have to stay within our class."

"Mitzi and Daniel are in our class. So's Betsy and --

"Not that kind of class, dopey. Social class. Maybe Joseph's a peon, too. Anyway, he's Spanish and Catholic. Cora Jean's a Dago. Dagos, kikes, peons, Chinks, bohunks -- they're not like us, you know."

"Is that why you never talk to anyone at school? You snub them on purpose? Just because they're not just like you?"

"And Martin's a cracker. We stay away from crackers, too."

"Well, not me. Mother doesn't -- " Oh-oh. Mother often told me to keep away from Mitzi. But that was because she was fresh-mouthed, too smart for her own good, and spoiled rotten by too much allowance. Wasn't it?

"No, not from you. I'm allowed to encourage you. You're Swedes, but you're not bohunk Swedes. Mother says your family's on the plain side, but you're not common. Besides, you have a family tragedy, and I'm supposed to let it teach me Christian charity for your poor little idiot sister."

I stood up to stare at her. What was she nattering about?

"Did you see any lice?"

"Lice?"

"In Pedro's hair. I kept hoping I'd see some."

Dorie and Noreen ran up, panting and grinning. I grabbed Dorie's hand. "We're going home."

Over my shoulder, Roberta's voice chased me. "But it's early. You can't go home yet. PEGGY! IF YOU GO, WE'LL HAVE TO GO TOO."

"THAT'S YOUR PROBLEM. NOT MINE."

It felt so good to shout at her that I stopped for a moment, turned around, and shouted it again.

40

I beelined for the dictionary. Family offered nothing new; tragedy brushed by "a mournful or fatal event" to dwell at length on stage dramas. Baffled, I checked to see if the two words, together, meant something else. Dead end.

It handled kike and Chink briefly -- a Jew; a Chinese -- but had lots to say about peon, including "a member of the laboring class.... in southwestern states formerly a part of Mexico, a person bound to service for payment of a debt." I had to go to the seventh definition of cracker: "One of the lower class of the white population of the southern United States ... inhabiting the hills or backwoods."

Nothing about lise or lice and nothing about Swedes that counted. Under bohunk I found, "a laborer, usually unskilled, esp. one from the former empire of Austria-Hungary; a Bohemian, a Slovak, a Magyar, or a Croatian." I knew laborer from Sunday school, so what on earth could be so shameful about that?

Under Dago, I found "used chiefly in contempt"; contempt was "the feeling with which one regards that which is esteemed mean, vile, worthless."

Pretty Cora Jean Rossi, mean, vile, or worthless? (For goodness sake! She'd starred as Mary in our Christmas pageant.) That smart Betsy ... perky Mitzi ... funny, silly Daniel.... What did those bad names have to do with them? And Martin lived in a big brick house on Royal Court....

How could Roberta be so blind? So mean?

Comforted, I looked up idiot: "an unlearned, ignorant, or simple person.... Idiot ... implies absence, commonly congenital, of intellectual or reasoning powers; it is often less strictly used to characterize someone who is felt to have acted with utter stupidity." I'd planned to check out congenital, but when I got to the synonyms -- fool, simpleton, blockhead, dolt; all of them familiar -- I decided I knew enough already.

Chanting "Sticks and stones may break my bones," I followed my ears to Dorie. She was in front of Mother's three-panel mirror, admiring her skirt swirl as she sang and danced to "What a Friend We Have in Jesus." I moved in to swing and

sway with her. By the third chorus, I had my own version
almost worked out:

> "What a friend I have in Webster's,
> Tum te tum te tum we bear.
> How I love my dictionary,
> All I need to know is there."

Thanks to Webster's, I now knew that prissy, stuck-up
Roberta had a big dirty mouth. She was the poor little idiot,
calling people names who had done her no harm....

"Peggy! Telephone!"

It was almost suppertime. Dorie and I were playing roly-
poly on the sidewalk in front of our house with Harriet and
Alice. Who else ever phoned me?

"It's Roberta. Don't keep her waiting."

Oh boy -- humble pie?

I finished my turn, took my time in getting to the wall phone
in the staircase hall. Should I be sour like Jane Withers, or sweet
like Shirley Temple?

"She thanked me for the handkerchief box," said Mother.
"Your little friend has perfect manners."

Sour, I decided. "What do you want? I was outside
playing."

Mother shook a be-polite finger, hovered in the front room.
Roberta's voice was so small I could barely hear her.

"I'm really sorry I made you mad -- or hurt your feelings."

"You didn't."

"You're not mad at me?"

"Well.... " It was hard to be sour with Mother listening,
harder still to stay mad at that tiny, shaking voice. "Don't you
think I should be?"

"I apologize. I'm so sorry I said that. You won't tell on me,
will you?"

"Of course not." But which "that" was she sorry for?

"Then I'll see you tomorrow. Let's meet at recess, okay?"

"You mean talk together at school?" She was always
confusing me; that wasn't what I wanted to say at all. Could I

whisper -- sharp, stern, driving a hard bargain -- that meanwhile she should clean up her dirty mouth? What came out instead surprised me: "We're <u>all</u> laborers in our Father's vineyard. Remember?"

It surprised her too. "Sure," she said after a minute. "I know that.... Or maybe lunch?"

"Each and every one. Mitzi and Cora Jean and Dorie and --"

"Okay, okay. You're right, and I'm sorry. Can you eat lunch at school tomorrow?"

"No. Mother makes me come --" A light bulb flashed in my head. "I'll ask her tonight." The flash also reminded me that it was probably a very good time to show off some good manners. "Thanks a lot for calling. That was a wonderful birthday party. Mother says the bath salts are really classy."

Mother was on the couch, smiling. Laughing, maybe. At what?

"Roberta wants me to eat lunch at school tomorrow. Can I?"

"Well, we'll see. You don't think that life with a best friend is getting too rich for your blood?"

Ho ho ho, I thought, galloping outdoors -- a crusading knight with two victories behind, a third one ahead. Mother's "We'll see" almost always blossomed into a "Yes"; Roberta's white flag was mine to flaunt; and I could almost touch the bright red twenty-six-inch Elgin bicycle that was steadily wheeling my way.

Mother was right. Overnight, life was overwhelmingly rich-- rich with action, change, daily surprise. "You almost need a date book these days," she said. It was almost true. Twice a week or so, I ate lunch at school; on the other days Roberta, bubbling over with every step, joined me on the home-for-lunch walk.

"Why not walk all the time?" I asked, wondering why she hadn't figured it out for herself. "Why let Sophie drive you?"

"Most afternoons I have to go places. On Mondays I have my piano lesson, and on Tuesdays and Fridays I go to the library, and some Wednesdays it's the dentist, and --"

"The library? What for?"

"To get a new book. I read two a week. Want to go with me?"

I nodded yes, and Mother said yes, so twice a week Sophie took us to the neighborhood library. We browsed until each chose a book -- books so wondrous strange (like <u>The</u> <u>Secret</u> <u>Garden</u> and <u>Anne</u> <u>of</u> <u>Green</u> <u>Gables</u> and a series on children of faraway lands) that I blushed over my crush on the big-little books. A week into our public friendship, Roberta joined our Campfire group; the meetings not only took care of our Thursday afternoons but also led to regular trips downtown to Campfire headquarters for beads, scarves, pamphlets, anything we could think of.

Po-faced, the popcorn-wagon gang eyed Sophie's pickup service -- muttering, I was sure, about prissy prigs and royal maids.

"Why don't we go by streetcar?" I said, the second time we went downtown. "We could catch the Montavilla at the Circle, and ride home with Daddy."

"Could we really? Do you know how?" She'd never been on a bus or streetcar, had never even thought of such a thing. "I'll ask tonight."

Her mother agreed as fast as mine did these days.

"Oh wow," said Roberta, when the jolting streetcar slithered us from side to side on its slick seats, or when we had to sprint for the bus that would take us to the library. "Talk about fun!"

"See what you've been missing without me?" I said, pretending I'd known all along what fun it was.

One night while I was again telling Dorie the Rapunzel story, I sat straight up in bed, struck by the lightning of a brand new thought: Roberta <u>had</u> been a prisoner after all -- a beautiful but lonely princess hidden away deep in the forest, pining away in a gray stone tower, pretending to be a queen. That made <u>me</u> the valiant prince who had, magically, known she was there, and who rode over hill and dale to come bravely to her rescue....

"Pah okay?" asked Dorie, sitting up too.

"Oh yes, Dorie. Pah's a <u>prince</u>. A truly valiant prince."

If Dorie missed our lunches or play-school sessions, she made up for them in her own way. Every day radio music blared out from our house; on the porch, she grabbed my hands to whoosh me through the rooms in a wild and wonderful dance -- spinning, jumping, stomping, until we dropped to the floor in a wiggling, giggling, gasping heap. What fun! I thought, surprised again.

Another bulb flashed in my head the night before my birthday party. Was I wearing out the word surprise? Alarmed, I headed to Webster's for a reserve supply of synonyms: startle, perplex, bewilder; overwhelm, awe, shock; take unawares, strike with wonder; astonish, amaze, astound....

Talk about rich, I thought, tasting each delicious word on my tongue. Talk about <u>rich</u>. Carefully, one by one, I picked them up, turned them over, and stored them deep in my heart, sure that they would last forever.

IV.
UNTOWARD TRAVAIL

The changes that arrived with my birthday bicycle rode in as surely and sweetly as summer itself. For the first couple of weeks, rain or shine, Roberta and I practiced daily on the sidewalk, with Dorie chasing alongside. "Doh's legs are wheels," she said, shaking her head whenever I invited her to try riding. Because her tears flowed each time Roberta or I fell, we learned in record time and were soon racing in the street.

"You know your boundaries," said Mother, every time I headed out. "From the park to Glisan, from Twenty-eighth to Thirty-ninth. We can trust you, can't we?"

For several weeks they could; even those blocks bloomed with intrigue when viewed from the seat of a speeding bike. But when no-coat weather came, we launched our Saturday Adventures. With snacks, a book, a cushion, and a flashlight in each basket, we sailed off at eight o'clock for Far Horizons and Parts Unknown. Valuing surprise over boss-hood, I was content to let Roberta pick the destination, schedule our activities, and mastermind an equipment list that expanded as our range widened.

Our first forbidden destination was school. We crawled under the fence into the eerily empty grounds -- not too eerie for us, we decided, but too empty, with no plants to hide us from the blinkless windows nearby. On the next Saturday we penetrated the wasteland around the railroad tracks off Forty-fifth. Alive with brambles that bloodied our legs, disappointingly empty of trains and hobos, it seemed no true Eden either.

"This might be it," we agreed when we discovered the wooded tract some twenty blocks up Burnside, towards Montavilla. In the deep shade and dense undergrowth -- "Surely the forest primeval, at the end of the Oregon trail" -- we could neither see nor hear passing traffic.

47

Said Roberta, our wise and foresighted leader: "Next time we'll bring knives to blaze some trails. Otherwise we could get lost in here for days."

Said I, our wise and respected sidekick: "But we can't come here every time -- at least not yet. We must continue our quest. We must continue adventuring westward ho."

Once we were there, wherever there was, the Adventure could unfold. First we hid our bikes, even from each other. ("If we're fallen upon by thieves, one of us can go for help," said Roberta. "And if they resort to torture, neither of us will know all.") Then, flashlights in hand, we circled the area together, establishing our territory, Roberta said, in the manner of wild beasts. Next we separated to investigate the inner terrain, hooting in code now and then to prove that all remained well. Finally, "despite trial, tribulation, and untoward travail," we triumphantly reunited to exchange tales of remarkable events -- Indian uprisings, animal attacks, flash floods -- and to lead each other to such special sightings as wolf lairs, burial grounds, watering holes, and traces of old ghost towns.

Pioneering accomplished, we settled on our cushions, shared our snacks, and took turns reading aloud. From this reading we selected a drama of the week that we acted out until it was time to go home for lunch.

"Well, I'm glad you're with a girl as responsible as Roberta," said Mother each time I stoutly refused to tell her exactly where we'd been. "Secrets are fun, I know, but just remember we trust you not to do anything foolish."

I knew well what "foolish" included: riding on busy streets, going to deserted spots, leaving our bikes unguarded, talking to strangers, going too far from home. I also now knew, from watching Roberta, a surefire formula for diverting grown-ups: Give thanks at every opportunity, and always look humble.

"Oh, Mother, thanks so much for understanding."

With school out, we went several times a week. Taking lunch opened up new horizons: Mount Tabor Park, Rocky Butte, Fremont, Montavilla -- even downtown, though I worried that one father or the other might spot us; it was their territory, after all.

"Not Farmers' Market. They never go there. I dare you."

Until my birthday party, Roberta knew nothing of the market. "We order our flowers from Tommy Luke," she'd said, wrinkling her nose at the heart-stopping explosion of daffodils on the green-for-Saint-Patrick tablecloth. "They say it best with roses."

"Oh yeah? Well, Mother gets our flowers by the armful at Farmers' Market." All at once I was burstingly proud, of Mother and of the hard-working prayers Dorie and I always put in to get daffodils into bloom by my party. "Yesterday there wasn't a daffodil in sight, but Mother didn't give up. She went again this morning, and there they were. A miracle! Just for my birthday!"

"Oh wow," said Roberta, hugging me. "What's Farmers' Market? Can I go with you sometime?"

It was on the riverfront, on the seedy fringes of downtown; we often walked to it from Campfire headquarters, so I resisted her dare. "Where would we hide our bikes? Besides, our Adventures are supposed to be wilderness, not civilization."

To my relief, she agreed. I had a secret problem: money.

In civilization Roberta expected me to buy things -- gum, cones, comic books, little presents -- as freely as she did. But she got an allowance of fifty cents a week and I got none at all. Mother didn't mind giving me carfare or change for special treats, but wouldn't hear of giving me a regular allowance. "Why should I dole out spending money to burn a hole in your pocket?"

The Northrups paid us ten cents a pail for weeding their lawn. Could I keep it secret from Mother? Too risky, I decided, and instead begged humbly to keep it for spending.

"Well, it's against my own better judgment. In fact, I'll hire you girls too. But don't you forget, miss, that you're part of our family team. Don't start pushing to be paid for your household chores."

It took almost an hour to fill a pail -- boring, uncomfortable work. With every tenth weed, I tossed in dirt or rocks.

"You're cheating too often," said Roberta one day. I blushed, caught red-handed. "The trick is don't overdo it. Soil and rocks weigh too much. Dead leaves look accidental, and don't rattle."

Most weeks we filled five pails, earning a quarter each. A dime of that for Dorie, I decided. Hush money? I'd squirmed as Roberta told me how to cheat better, hoping Dorie wasn't listening. In vain. She threw in leaves every time I did.

"Dorie, I'm on the horns of another dilemma," I whispered from my bed one night. "If I say 'Roberta's allowed,' or 'Roberta has one,' Mother usually comes through. But she hates allowances. That's what first set her against Mitzi -- that day at the drugstore when she saw Mitzi get a Lucky Mondae just before dinner. Remember? 'Why do parents put temptation in a child's path?' she says. So maybe I'd be dumb to tell her about Roberta's allowance? What if she starts picking on her?"

Talking to Dorie always helped; sometimes I didn't quite know what was in my head until it spilled out of my mouth. "Mother's not nearly as strict with me now that Roberta's my best friend."

"Pah? Doh wants to ask." She dropped my hand, sat up. "If Rahtah is Pah's best friend ... is Doh Pah's best friend too?"

Oh dear me. Was Dorie feeling left out? I got out of bed to hug her. "Oh Dorie. You're not just my best friend. You're my best best friend. Plus that you're my sister. You're the very best sister in the whole wide world."

She laughed out loud, hugged back hard. A few minutes later, as we slipped off to sleep, she gave my hand a little squeeze.

"Pah is Doh's best best sister too."

All summer long, a procession of ripening fruit -- cherries, plums, apricots, pears, apples -- lured us into the yards of empty houses or into vacant lots throughout the neighborhood. Roberta scaled the trees to pick the treasures; I stayed at the bottom with a sack to fill. If Roberta noticed that I seldom left the ground, she was too polite to say so.

When the trees were nearby, one or both of our little sisters came along. For the first few times, Dorie sat near the tree, watching Roberta scoot around the branches.

"Rahtah's a monkey," she laughed, wiggling in admiration.

Then one day when we were picking plums at the empty corner house, Dorie erupted. She yelled, "Doh's a monkey too," pulled off her shoes and socks, and scampered up the trunk.

"No, Dorie!" I yelled, going up after her. Two branches up I froze solid, too terrified either to look down or go up. "HELP!"

"You're on your own, Peggy," said Roberta. "Sink or swim."

I'm the wrong shape for it, I mourned, and chose to sink.

Safely on the ground, I screamed again. "Roberta, help her down. SHE DOESN'T KNOW HOW TO CLIMB TREES." A few minutes of watching told me that was an out-and-out lie; Dorie was as much at home up there, flitting around the branches, as a bird.

They finally came down, breathless with laughter. "Rah rah for Doh," said Roberta several times on the walk home. "Peggy, aren't you proud of her?"

I was a puddle of sweat, that's what I was.

"Pah, can Doh tell Mah and Dah?"

What kind of big sister was I? First a coward in danger, and now a coward who wanted to keep Dorie's hidden talent hidden.

"Oh Dorie, I am proud of you. You were wonderful. But --"

"Can Doh tell?"

"Yes, we have to tell. But let's keep it secret until dinner, okay? Then you can tell Mother and Daddy at the same time."

By dinnertime she was almost beside herself, and I understood things better. Tapping my glass with a spoon, I managed to raise a big-enough smile. "Listen now. Hear ye. Dorie has something really exciting to tell you."

She stood up, took a little bow. "Doh has a big surprise. Doh climbs tree like a monkey."

Daddy put down his fork. Mother looked at me. "She climbed a tree? Peggy, where were you?"

"Right there. Admiring her. She was wonderful."

51

Daddy clapped his hands noiselessly. "Good for you, Dorie. And you didn't fall?"

"No. Doh knows how. Doh brave."

Mother clapped a little too. "We're proud of you for not being scared." She stabbed me with an I-want-to-speak-to-you-this-very-instant look, and I trailed her into the kitchen.

"Mother, you wouldn't have believed it. She --"

"I can't believe what I'm hearing. You know better than --"

"I know I failed her. But you have to see it to believe it. Can we all walk over to the plum tree after dinner?" I put my finger on her lips. "Please Mama? Trust me?"

"Mama" almost never slipped out; it always startled both of us. A long, scary, staring moment ... then she nodded.

With Dorie skipping in front of us, I walked between Mother and Daddy, explaining. "It happened so fast I couldn't stop her.

I didn't even know she wanted to. Well, you'll see."

Dorie and I sat on the ground, as we had that afternoon. "Okay, Dorie. Now do just exactly what you did before."

"I don't think I can stand to watch this," said Mother, moving close to Daddy to hold hands. Dorie zipped up the trunk, danced from limb to limb, laughing with each graceful, fearless move.

"My God," whispered Daddy. "Look at that girl move."

"Oh good heavens," said Mother. "When did she learn how?

They sank down beside me in the overgrown grass to watch.

"How can we find the heart to stop her?" said Mother. "Peggy, did you tell her she was safer without her brogues?"

"No. I didn't have time to tell her <u>anything</u>. She just knew, I guess, that bare feet are more like Keds."

She didn't come down until it was almost dark. We all hugged her at once. "Doh teach Pah," she said, from seventh heaven. "Pah can go to tree school with Doh."

Mother bought her some Keds the next day, and little by little Dorie got me up almost every tree in the neighborhood. By apple time, I could go almost as high as she and Roberta did, but, like Noreen, I liked it best close to the trunk.

"I'm proud of you, Peggy," said our brave-hearted leader.

"Thanks a lot," said our lily-livered sidekick, truly grateful for her praise, for Dorie's teaching, and for the fact that fruit season was finally coming to an end.

"Why don't you ever invite Roberta to Sunday supper?" Mother asked several times during the summer.

We often ate at each other's houses, but I wasn't yet ready to trust Roberta with our family games night. What if she sniffed at our peasant food? Or was bored by our word games? Or -- worst of all -- made fun of Daddy's English workbooks?

Then, one October Sunday, Mother invited her to "stay on for supper." While Roberta phoned for permission, I chased Mother into the kitchen. "How could you do that to me? She's my friend to invite or not."

Mother put her finger on my lips. "Trust me, child. She'll love it -- you'll see."

"Cornflakes?" Roberta whispered when she saw the box in the middle of the kitchen table. "Cornflakes for dinner?"

Mother smiled. "It's supper, not dinner. An old-fashioned farm supper. On farms, people eat their big meal at noon to give them energy for the afternoon's work."

Roberta ate two heaping bowlfuls. "I love it. I just love it," she said, every time she spelled a word right, or joined Dorie's cheering squad. "Can I come every Sunday?"

Dorie clapped, Daddy grinned, Mother winked at me, and I reached over to give Roberta a great big happy squeeze.

Later that week she invited me to my first Saturday night dinner party. "Wear a party dress, but expect to be surprised."

The surprise: We were the hired help. In lacy aprons, we passed nuts and olives to the six grown-ups as they sat around the fireplace with tall, pretty drinks. We ate in the kitchen. Sophie served us, but whenever a bell rang from the dining room we jumped up to carry things to and from the candlelit table.

"We've had the same candles on our dining room table for years," I said. "Mother never lights them."

"That's because your family never has dinner parties."

53

Vaguely, I wondered why not. "Well, your family doesn't even own a dictionary," I said, in case she was insulting us.

"All the better to beat you to yours, my dear," she said, and we both had to laugh, remembering our races.

Roberta gave me twelve cents of the quarter she got for helping. Reluctantly, I told Mother about our salaries, but I knew better than to tell her we didn't help with the dishes. ("That's Sophie's job," said Roberta, aghast. "We'd lose face.")

"Penny saved, penny earned," said Mother every time I pushed my coins into my Save-and-Earn bank. Dorie and I each had one. Leather-covered, they looked like books but couldn't be opened; the downtown bank had the key. Reminding her that she'd let me spend my weed earnings might backfire, so I sulked only a bit. "It's not fair. I've already earned it."

A few days later, while Mother was shopping, I spent twenty minutes in the den closet with my bank, persuading a coin to slide out on a knife. It's not stealing, I told myself; it's my own hard-earned money. But the sneaked-out dime seemed to burn a guilty hole in my shoe until I spent it on three U-No bars: one for Dorie, one for Roberta, and only one for me, just in case God was paying any attention to what I was up to these busy days.

For Christmas, Mother and Daddy gave the house a baby grand piano. Dorie and I were as thrilled as they were.

"Can I have piano lessons?" I begged, plunking away at the keys. "Please please pretty please?"

"Soon we'll play duets," I told Roberta Monday afternoons as we separated for music lessons. Soon, instead, I hated my weekly hour of insults from Mrs. Glassner: "Your fingers are sticks"; "You plod like an elephant"; "Are your ears full of wax?" I also hated my daily hour of practice. Dorie sat beside me, pretending to imitate any tune or chord I trickled out, but tunes and chords were few and far between.

"Can't I quit?" I begged every week, almost in tears.

"No. You'll be happy later that you stuck with it."

I deserve a reward for obedience, I told myself regularly as I headed for my bank, knife in hand. Or: If Mother lets me quit piano lessons, I'll quit stealing from myself. Or, most often: It's my money to spend; the future can take care of itself.

"A dictionary!" breathed Roberta, eyes sparkling.

"A <u>dictionary</u>?" snorted Pauline. "What kind of dopey present is that?"

We were again at the Orange Lantern, watching Roberta open her birthday presents.

"It's not just a dictionary," I said. "Read the inscription." I was proud of it, though I owed the basic idea to an advertisement for encyclopedias.

Roberta read it aloud. "'For my dear friend, Roberta -- an Adventure-filled path to an open mind.' Oh, Peggy, that's really beautiful. I'll treasure it forever and ever."

"Heavens to Betsy," said one of the twins, making a face at the others. "You're both nuts."

Roberta sat up straight, looked around. All four girls were laughing at us; I patted my hat, glad that it matched my dress this time. "Oh yeah?" she said. "Well, I have an announcement to make. Today's an anniversary for Peggy and me. We've been best friends for exactly a year."

Poor Bean, I thought, dazzled.

Only one thing dimmed the glory of that day: all the table talk about Roberta's family moving to the Heights soon.

"Oh, that doesn't mean anything," she said afterwards. "We've been talking about moving there for years. Now the house next door to Bean's might be for sale this summer."

"You never told me."

She shrugged. "Mother always says don't count on it."

"Do you want to move?"

"Of course not. I used to, but not any more. Besides, we're expecting a new brother next summer, so I'm safe now. Mother's too busy fixing up a nursery to think about moving." She slapped her hand over her mouth. "I forgot -- that's a secret."

"A new brother? How do you get a new brother?"

"You won't tell I forgot? You'd really get me in dutch."

"Of course not. How do you get a new brother?"

"We aren't sure yet that it's a boy, of course."

"Roberta! How do you get a new baby?"

"It just comes. It's a blessing from heaven."

I knew there was more to it than that, and was disappointed she didn't. I told her about Kitty Kelly, and out of wedlock, and illegitimate babies.

"That's impossible," she said. "People can't have babies unless they're married. That's because it takes a daddy to plant the seed."

"Plant the seed? How?"

She'd never thought to ask.

"Well, ask!" I said, stomping my foot. "It's something we need to know."

"Why should I ask my mother? Why don't you ask yours?"

"You know perfectly well my mother won't talk about things like that. And besides, it's your mother who's having a baby. She's the one who remembers how."

Again, the daffodils bloomed just in time for my birthday.

Roberta gave me an atlas, inscribed "For my best friend Peggy. A bigger look at Far Horizons and Parts Unknown."

Thrilled, I read it aloud, then tapped my glass. "Hear ye. Hear ye one and all." I stood·up. "I want to announce that Roberta and I have been best friends for over thirteen months now." As everyone else clapped, a glum Harriet jutted her chin straight out. I knew why: Her class was pairing off, and she was refusing to get stuck with Alice. Poor Harriet; I didn't blame her. Who'd want to be best friends with a girl whose favorite words were "Don't be childish" and "Icky. That's horrid"?

But lucky me. Roberta and I had so many favorite words that, at the rate we were going, we'd soon be word millionaires.

"Some people collect stamps," said Roberta as we worked out our rules. "We collect words, and we do it honorably." That meant we couldn't skim them from Webster's; we had to catch them one by one. They didn't have to be brand new, but had to offer some special charm. Some -- cantankerous, befuddlement, discriminate, haphazard, lollipop -- skittered playfully on the tongue; others -- dog, civil, brake, shake, full -- hid unexpected meanings; others -- pickle, grope, lump, glob, squirm, gargle, bloat, squatter -- were so ugly they were lovable.

"And treat them honorably too," said I. That meant we had to exercise them daily. Webster's provided the definitions; at first we kept tallies as we trotted out each word in each meaning and form, but they came in too fast after we branched out.

One branch: our Gift Lists. Roberta collected P words for me; I collected R ones for her. R had its charmers -- romp, risque, robust, ramparts, rambunctious, ragamuffin, rollicking, rutabaga, rapscallion, ripple, raffish -- especially after we voted to accept proper nouns like Rumpeltstiltskin and Rotterdam. But P thrilled me pink: pelican, pharoah, peninsula, profound, phoney, phantom, predicament, poliomyelitis, pus, pettifoggery, perpendicular, Pago Pago, puny, paucity, petulant, plop, pestiferous, pox, putter, propinquity, pugnacious, percolator, paraphernalia, prenuptial, pumpernickel, pitter-patter....

"It's profoundly unfair," I complained. "It's _my_ initial, and you get all the fun of landing them."

"Well, you get to help play with them, don't you?"

We also specialized in natural pairs, like mixed blessings, conflicting emotions, untoward travail, living death, common humanity, human condition, open mind, perpetual motion, wishful thinking, balancing act, soup kitchen, blessed event, amazing grace.... Once we started to notice them, they showed up everywhere, each more valuable than the last.

"I think we should title them Popular Pals," said Roberta. "Or do you like Particular Pals better?"

"How about Cherished Chums?"

"Or Cooperative Comrades?"

"Or Bosom Buddies?"

"Oh wow. Or Favorite Friends -- like us."

"Better and better. Or maybe --"

"I know! Sympathetic Sisters. That's even more like us."

"Perfect. Sweet, simple, silly, sympathetic sisters."

"Sweet, simple, silly, sympathetic, secret, subterranean, subtle, sappy, solemn as Solomon...."

That was the kind of best friend to have -- someone who kept you on your toes every minute. Why, I hadn't even known that I'd wanted an atlas until Roberta gave it to me. Patting it, smelling it, flipping through its colorful pages, I wondered if this was how she'd felt about the handkerchief box.

"The time has come for us to pledge our allegiance to each other in blood," said Roberta one night from her cot.

At her house, we slept in cots on their sleeping porch; at ours, we stayed in my bed until Dorie fell asleep, then moved into the twin beds in the spare room.

"Oh, maybe not. Why don't we just swear on a Bible?"

"It's not good enough. Unless we exchange blood, we don't really become blood sisters. And to make our bond last forever, we have to do it outside, in the dead of night, when the moon is full and the wolves are howling."

"Tonight's the night," we declared, weekend after weekend. We kept ourselves awake by arguing about where to draw the blood, and what to do with it once we had it.

"We'll puncture each other's right thumbs," said Roberta. "Then we'll rub our thumbs together, and make crosses on each other's foreheads."

"I'd rather pick at a scab," I said, because I always had a fresh supply of them. "And we should make the crosses on the bottom of our feet. Otherwise we'll have to wash them off by morning -- before they have time to age properly."

When the night finally felt dead enough, we sneaked down the stairs, hand in hand and barefoot, and ventured out into the dark, cold, rustling yard.

"I don't think the moon's full enough, do you? It won't take for all eternity unless the moon's completely full."

"Not many wolves out, either."

"But if it isn't a wolf, what's that noise?"

We never stayed to find out.

Roberta just rolled her eyes when I asked her, week after week, what she'd found out about baby seeds.

"I bet your mother didn't tell you anything," I said finally.

"Oh yes she did, but I'm not allowed to tell you something your parents don't want you to know."

We were in the den, looking up words. It was my turn at the big dictionary; Roberta was browsing through the bookshelves.

"Hey, look at this," she said, excited. "Here's what a baby looks like before it's born."

I knew what she'd found: one of Mother's old textbooks, called <u>Obstetrics</u> <u>for</u> <u>Nurses</u>. I jumped up, knocked it out of her hand.

"If you won't tell me what your mother said about seeds, I won't let you look at my mother's book. Fair is fair."

"Well, she didn't say much -- only that a daddy has a certain little apparatus for planting seed, and when the time is ripe he plants the seed in a mommy's pocket."

"Her pocket? What pocket?"

She didn't know. Maybe the book would tell us? We pored over it -- sickening drawings of little frogs growing into babies -- but found nothing about a daddy's apparatus or a mommy's pocket.

Our car hummed up the drive. "Quick! Hide the book!" Glancing around the room for telltale evidence, I spotted a tiny envelope on the floor. Dropped in the scuffle? Flushing, I stuffed it in my sock, where it remained, forgotten, until I undressed for bed.

The card inside, edged in flowers, carried a poem and three lines filled in with Mother's round handwriting:

> She fills our hearts with happiness,
> We know the Angels brought her.
> And all our future days she'll bless,
> Our brand new Baby Daughter.
> Weight: 6 pounds, 5 ounces
>
> Date: July 12, 1924
> Name: Dorothy Anne

Smiling, I started to put it in my shoe as a morning reminder to return it to the book. Oh-oh, I thought; something's fishy. I looked again: 1924. How could that be? I was born in 1926, and

Dorie was two years younger. The envelope was stamped "Return to sender." The postmark said July 16, 1924.

In bed, singing, my tongue felt like a rock. When Dorie finally fell asleep, I tiptoed out to the light in the hall. The card and the envelope still said 1924. Impossible, I decided at last; it was simply a mistake that couldn't be explained. I was the big sister; it was my job to keep my little sister's path clear of pits, snares, and stumbling blocks. That I knew as well as my own name, and nothing in the world could change it.

But sleep didn't come. Mother and Daddy came up to bed; the downstairs clock chimed eleven ... eleven-fifteen ... eleven-thirty.... At midnight I gave up, got up. In the dark kitchen, I found an empty tin can in the trash under the sink, reached for the wooden matches on the stove.

There! I whispered, watching the paper brown, curl, and crumble into ashes.

There! I whispered again, burying it, can and all, in the bottom of the outside garbage pail.

There! I whispered again, safely back in my bed. The birth announcement was gone, and I could forget all about that strange and frightening and absolutely impossible mystery.

A couple of weeks later: Black Friday.

One by one, I removed nine pennies from my bank, pushed the knife in for one more -- and the cupboard was bare.

It couldn't be.

But it was.

From my secret notes in Volume X of the Harvard Classics, I learned that I had squandered, coin by coin, four dollars and fifty-seven cents in less than six months. A fortune. All gone.

The true disaster hit me that night in bed. One day Mother would pick up my bank, shake it, and know the terrible terrible terrible truth: The only burglar who would burgle a kid's bank was the kid herself. "Oh, Dorie, I'm really in for it now."

The first time I was alone, I grabbed the bank and a small garden spade, flew to the strip of ground behind the garage. Half an hour's hard work swallowed up the bank forever. In the process I unearthed three pennies and a nickel that Harriet and I had buried when we were young, silly, carefee -- innocent.

They were a good omen, I was sure. To prove I'd learned my lesson, I'd put these and all future coins into Dorie's bank. As added insurance, I kept my fingers crossed all day, chanting "I hope I hope I hope I hope." If I was very lucky, and very, very, very good, Mother wouldn't notice that one bank was missing until I was grown up, married, and safely living next door to Roberta on the street of Far Horizons and Parts Unknown.

V.
SHE-BEARS AND OTHER CREATURES

In our Campfire group's May doughnut sale, Roberta and I tied for fourth place. No coincidence; we'd gone from door to door together, then split the orders. She shrieked happily when she saw our prize: a booklet called "How to Be a Good Camper."

"It's an omen," she said. "We're destined to be buddies at Camp Namanu this summer. Wouldn't that be wonderful?"

I wasn't sure; Mother wasn't either. She called Mrs. Northrup, came back smiling. "Well, she's all for it."

The only vacancies left were for the first two weeks of July. "Good timing," said Mother. "That's when their baby's due."

"I'd miss the Fourth of July."

"They have Fourth of July at camp."

"And Dorie's birthday -- I'd miss that too."

"We'll celebrate a few days late. Don't you want to go?"

"Of course I want to go. And Roberta has to have a buddy."

"Well, think it over. Maybe you're still too young for it."

"I'm not either." But by morning I'd remembered something else. "I'd miss the wedding -- Miss Sarah's."

Mother laughed. "You'd also miss two weeks of Grandpa."

"Oh goody, would I really?"

At camp, some hours raced by; others dragged. I loved the shows we staged, the canoe paddling, and the evening songfests around a bonfire. I hated the mosquitoes, the endless blister-raising hikes to nowhere, and most of all the daily swimming; everyone else in our cabin was a tadpole, trying for frog, and I wasn't even a polliwog yet.

"You know, you could be talking about either mixed blessings or conflicting emotions," mused Roberta as we lay on our bare cots during Hush-Hush Hour. "Which label works best?"

"How about mixed emotions?" As we laughed, I realized that my feelings about Hush-Hush Hour had changed from one unmixed into another unmixed. At first I'd hated taking a daily rest; now -- with quiet talk allowed -- I welcomed the semiprivacy it gave us to work on the Adventure book we planned to write together.

One afternoon, while we elaborated and collaborated, Edith the eavesdropper rose up on her elbow. "That's a lie. You couldn't possibly have heard a lion roar in Portland."

Roberta always held her own. "I didn't say it <u>was</u> a lion. I said it <u>sounded</u> like a lion."

"Pooh! You're both liars, with those stupid adventures."

"We're not either. We're only liars if we want you to believe us. We don't care if you believe us or not."

"Oh boy," I whispered. "You really and truly are profound."

"You really and truly are a baby," said Roberta, on the bus home on Saturday afternoon. "Only babies get homesick."

"I'm not either homesick. I just don't mind going home. Aren't you excited about seeing your new sister?"

"Of course I am, but I loved camp. Every minute of it."

"Well, I loved some minutes more than others. That's known as being discriminating."

Because she was going straight to the hospital, both fathers met the bus; we were both glad to get rid of each other for the day. At home our table was already celebrating: a bright blue tablecloth, our best china, and a huge bouquet of red and white roses from the back yard.

"Oh Mother, it's beautiful. Can I light the table candles?"

"It's broad daylight, child."

"So what? Atmosphere, Roberta says."

"Well ... go clean up for dinner. I bet you'll be happy to get out of those clothes."

Flickering candles welcomed us back to the table. Grandpa said a miraculously short grace, then opened his mouth only to eat as the rest of us chattered away about camp, the wedding, neighborhood news; he looked only mildly cranky when we sang "Happy Birthday" around Dorie's cake. It made me nervous.

"What's wrong with Grandpa?" I asked as we cleared off the dessert dishes. "He seems so -- so tame."

"Daddy told him he'd have to have a tray in his room unless he promised not to spoil tonight for us all."

"Wow."

"Wow is right. Daddy wants to show respect for his father, so it wasn't easy for him to talk that way to him."

"But Grandpa asks for --"

"That's enough. I have a homecoming surprise. You girls can go play until dark. Your gang's waiting to welcome you home."

At breakfast, huffing and puffing, Grandpa was back to normal.

When Dorie and I got the giggles over a piece of sausage bobbing up and down on his mustache, he called me a sinful Jezebel and told her she was an "abdomination to the Lord."

"You're excused, girls," said Daddy, slapping the table so hard that everything on it jumped.

Though it was time to go to Sunday school, I loitered at the dictionary, hoping to overhear fireworks. No luck, but I learned Jezebel was "a wicked, bold, or abandoned woman." Abdominal talked about stomachs and fish. Harmless, I decided, pleased again that even to smart Webster's Grandpa made no sense at all.

We scurried to our seats through a heavy silence. Roberta clutched my knee, pointed into her palm at the desk. In a black suit, with black hair skinned back into coronet braids, holding a pointer like a rifle against her shoulder, the new teacher stood guard, a stone-faced Major Hoople.

"And just who are you? Are you in the habit of being late?"

The clock on the wall said exactly ten o'clock, but I knew better than to argue. "Peggy Brandstrom, and this is --"

"Where are your manners? Stand up and do it right. This time answer my question."

I stood up. "I'm Peggy Brandstrom, and --"

"I'm Peggy Branson, Miss Garworth."

"I'm Peggy Branson, Miss Garworth, and this is my little sister Dorie. I'm sorry we're --"

"No excuses. Let your sister speak for herself."

Dorie looked at me, unsure. I nodded, gestured, and she stood up. "Doh is Doh," she said, beaming.

Miss Garworth's scowl stayed on Dorie. Could we sit down? When I started to, the scowl landed back on me.

"I've never set eyes on either of you, and this is my third Sunday. Are you in the habit of missing Sunday school?"

"No. I've --"

"No, Miss Garworth."

"No, Miss Garworth. I've been away at Camp Namanu."

"Camp, is it? Well, you've wasted enough of our time. We'll hear Bible verses now."

How could a bully teach Sunday school?

When it was my turn, I recited a verse I'd learned for Miss Sarah: "For verily I say unto you, That whosoever shall say unto this mountain, Be thou removed, and be thou cast into the sea; and shall not doubt in his heart, but shall believe that those things which he saith shall come to pass; he shall have whatever he saith." It seemed to go on forever. Wishing I'd chosen a shorter verse, I started to sit down.

"Hold on there for a moment, Peggy girl. Are you an empty-headed parrot? Have you any idea what those holy words mean?"

"Well, yes. That --"

"Have you pondered those words in your heart? Looked at them one by one, looking for the divine intention?"

"Yes, Miss Garworth. I think --"

"You think? I'm glad to hear you do think. All right then, let's hear from the tardy parrot who claims she can think."

Did she think she was smiling? If I was a parrot, she was a crocodile, baring her teeth as if I were her dinner.

"All it means is that faith moves mountains."

Miss Garworth lost her smile. "All it means? All it means? Am I to believe my ears?"

"Yes. No. Well, it means a lot, but it uses up a whole bunch of extra words to say something that's --"

"Extra words? You say the Bible wastes words?"

"No! You asked me if I'd thought about the meaning of each word. All those shall's and unto's and thou's don't count. Jesus is just telling us to believe in miracles."

Oh-oh. It was a mistake to bring Jesus into it. Turning red, Miss Garworth blew out her cheeks like the North Wind, ready to blast. I tried to get out of her way by sitting down.

"Oh no you don't. I'm not done with you yet."

Nor I with her, I discovered when I stood up; words just came rolling out on my outgoing tide. "What's more it's punctuated wrong. It needs quote marks, and has capitals and semicolons that don't belong. And there's an illegitimate which. It should be 'those things that come to pass,' not 'which come to pass,' because there aren't any commas to fence the which-words off."

Suddenly out of steam, I stuck my chin out as far as it would go, plunked into my chair as fast as possible, and felt the world come to a scarily noiseless stop. All the children stared up at the ceiling, or into a corner -- at anything safe they could find. Everyone except Dorie; her eyes, on me, were wide with worry. I wanted to say "Pah's okay," but dared only nod. She nodded back, tried hard to smile. When they finally came, Miss Garworth's slow, sharp words drummed like a March rain, relentlessly punishing a tin roof. "You get yourself back on your feet, little girl. Because you are now going to learn what happens to a child who dares to criticize Jesus in my class."

Standing again, I closed my eyes, hoping to find the sense to count to ten, or express thanks, or look humble. But I stomped my foot. "How could I be criticizing Jesus? He never wrote his words down. He didn't speak English, so those aren't even his own words. Someone else wrote that down, years and years later Miss Sarah said, and someone else translated it. It's like playing telephone -- everything gets garbled if too many peo--"

Miss Garworth crashed her pointer down on her desk. "SIT DOWN. YOU SIT DOWN THIS VERY MINUTE."

"JESUS WOULD HAVE KNOWN BETTER," I shouted back ... and sat.

Dorie's lower lip was out and trembling. When I shook my head, mouthed that I was okay, it pulled back a bit. A few minutes later, I could almost smile for her; as we sang "Onward Christian Soldiers," she got up to dance to its bouncing beat in the back of the room, all need for helpful tears forgotten.

"My oh my, I didn't know you had it in you," said Roberta as we headed for the park. "How you dared...."

"I shouldn't have. I'm supposed to show respect."

"You were great. Super. Wonderful. The old crow asked for it. She's even worse than your grandfather."

"She'll tell Mother. She might be calling right now."

All week, every time the phone rang, I braced for trouble.

Every time I came home, I felt Mother lying in wait, eyes aflame. On Thursday, when Daddy left for a two-week business trip, I relaxed a bit; at least it wouldn't be two to one. At Sunday breakfast, while Grandpa droned on, Mother snagged my eye, gestured. Sweating, I trailed her into the den closet, where she reached for her purse, dug into it, handed me two dimes.

"Peggy, I don't want you to ask questions. I wouldn't ask you to do this if I couldn't trust you to keep a secret." She gave me a great big hug. What on earth was going on?

"Take Dorie to the park, not to Sunday school. Or go to the drugstore for ice cream sodas, and then to the park afterwards with Roberta if you want. But Grandpa can't know you haven't been to Sunday school. Do you understand?"

I nodded, numb and dumb, and she hugged me again.

It was the longest hour of my life. Every few minutes Dorie asked, "Sunday school now?" What could I tell her?

I found a flexible lie: "We're on a dangerous secret mission." So we stalked the park paths, on the lookout for clues; escaped to the drugstore, foreign spies on our tail; whispered over our sodas, hatching clever schemes.... At long last, we lurked behind a shrub across the street from the church, scanning the horizon for allies from within.

Roberta came running. "Were you kicked out?"

"I don't know." I told her what had happened. "It's crazy. If Miss Garworth didn't tattle, we'd have gone as usual. If she did tattle, Mother would be mad. She wouldn't give me dimes, or say she trusted me, or look -- look so awfully <u>sad</u>."

"Maybe she's ashamed of you. Crying on the inside."

"No. She <u>hugged</u> me. Twice. She hardly ever hugs."

We worried all day, all week. If I tried to question Mother, she sighed a deep sigh. "We have to trust each other, child."

"Secret Mission, Chapter Two," I told Dorie the next Sunday.

"Doh wants Miss Sah."

"Ditto, Dorie. Ditto and double ditto."

I counted the days until Wednesday, when Daddy would come home. He and Mother would have lots to catch up on, once everyone else was in bed. With luck, a Listening-Post Operation would solve the mystery and end my misery.

To make sure I'd stay awake, I left my bed as soon as Dorie slipped off to sleep, sat on the floor near the door. Grandpa came lumbering up the stairs when the ten-o'clock news came on. Would he never get out of the bathroom? Never stop pacing his room? At last his bed creaked and his light went out.

The Richfield reporter was saying "That's thirty for tonight" as I entered the upstairs hall. Footsteps ... the radio snapped off. Holding my breath, I stood rigid, ready to run if they came straight upstairs. Ahhh. A rustling newspaper, the creak of the couch, a low murmur.... I edged downward slowly.

"Oh Anna, Anna. And Grandpa made it all the worse."

"Can you imagine his tantrums if he caught on? I felt like a criminal, sneaking phone calls to churches. What can we do now?"

"We'll think of something. Have you called them all?"

"Every church in northeast Portland -- like I did before. And I took her for two interviews. But she gets so quiet without her Peggy, and they think it's sulkiness. So no one wants her."

I blinked. What on earth --

"Oh, Axel, we can't let her world get any smaller."

Was she crying or mumbling? I slid down another step.

"You should have seen the woman. She sailed in here like a battleship the very day you left, all self-righteous bluster."

"Where was Grandpa?"

69

"In the basement painting, thank God. She actually enjoyed telling me Dorie didn't belong in Sunday school. 'For the sake of the others,' she said. 'I'm the good shepherd and must protect my little flock from such irreverence.' Can you imagine? A disruptive influence, she called her. Our quiet little Dorie!"

Dorie had been kicked out of Sunday school? DORIE?

"How? What had she done?"

"What she always does -- danced to the hymn." Big noisy sobs from Mother.... I swallowed, wiped my face with my pajama top.

"And our poor little confused Peggy!" Her sobs turned into a laugh, almost. "Oh, Axel, she's so worried. But what could I tell her? That her little sister isn't welcome in Sunday school anymore? You know how ferociously she protects her."

Daddy laughed softly. "Yeah. A real she-bear."

"There's more. Our Peg had to straighten the lady out on bad punctuation and an illegitimate which in her Bible verse."

Daddy laughed so loud that I jumped. "No kidding? She took on the Bible? Did she get kicked out too?"

"Oh no. The old battle-ax just wanted me to apologize for Peggy's bad behavior. Blasphemous behavior, she called it."

"She should meet Grandpa."

"What the stupid woman really wants is to save Peggy's soul from hellfire. I wish you'd seen her face when I just smiled and said we're very proud of Peggy's grasp of the English language."

"Good for you, Anna. And good for Peggy."

I could take their tears, and laughter, but considering my conscience -- squirming, screaming -- I couldn't take approval. Mindless of noise, I hightailed it to bed. A she-bear? Me? How could I ever be ferocious again if I could never stop crying?

"Last summer seemed twice as long," I complained to Roberta the day before school started.

"But this one was twice the fun." She touched my hand. "I'll never forget it. I hope you'll always remember that."

I tried to look properly solemn instead of glum and guilty. I hated hiding things from my best friend -- all those secrets and half-secrets, lies and half-lies. But I couldn't tell her about

Dorie. Feeling grubbier with each word, I'd said I'd messed up my Listening-Post Operation by falling asleep. A few days later I passed on Daddy's explanation: "We'd rather not expose you girls to Miss Garworth's kind of Christianity."

Roberta wasn't easily fooled. "But how did they know so soon what a beast she is? Who could have told them?"

"I don't know."

"Your father wasn't even home. How could he decide?"

"I don't know. Parents just know things, and decide things."

"Yeah, I guess they do."

After Grandpa left, the secret missions ended. On Sunday mornings, we took family rides -- often to Mt. Hood, shopping for a summer cabin. It should have been fun but wasn't, quite, because I suspected they were less interested in buying a cabin than in taking Dorie's mind off Sunday school. It didn't work. On Saturdays, Dorie still arranged our Sunday clothes; at night she asked from her bed, "Pah and Doh go to Sunday school tomorrow?"

One night a new answer popped out. "No, Dorie. We've graduated. We've gotten too big for Sunday school."

A long, worrisome silence.... Then she sat up in bed.

"Doh's too big for Sunday school too?"

I could hear the smile in her voice, so why did I want to cry?

At breakfast she tapped her glass, stood up grinning. "Pah says Doh's too big for Sunday school now."

"Hear that, Anna? She's happy she's outgrown Sunday school."

"Indeed I do. Rah rah for our two big girls." They both looked at me as if I were a Christmas angel. I couldn't smile back. It hurt too much to know so much and understand so little.

One Sunday in early November, the sun burst through the cold gray rain. Roberta called at nine o'clock. "Let's take the little girls to the park. Like we used to, in days of yore."

She'd told her parents about my run-in with Miss Garworth. "Oh no," I'd moaned, expecting Mrs. Northrup to blame me. But Mrs. Northrup yanked her girls out of Sunday school too. "No child has to take that sort of thing," she'd told Roberta.

"I still can't get over it," I said on the way to the play park. "I didn't think your mother liked me much."

"Don't be silly. She's dotty over you. Says you're the most responsible child she's ever met. And did you know that she told your mother about baby Elizabeth right from the start?"

"No! You mean they talk to each other? They're friends?"

"Not friends like us, but they talk on the phone a lot."

Was that just one more wriggling worry to add to the fat world of worries I was balancing in the air these secret-crammed days?

"Can we go feed the ducks?" asked Noreen, a couple of hours later. "I brought bread."

We strolled down Thirty-ninth to the pond, settled on the last empty bench. "Peggy, let's play Juan and Juanita in the bushes. Last chance of the year, probably."

"Now? Leave Dorie and Noreen here alone?"

"Alone? There are the Rossis, and the Dailey boys, and that's Betsy's family picnicking. It's as safe as Couch Street."

Juan and Juanita, our favorite book, gave us an ongoing hide-and-seek game of jungle survival. "Okay. I'm Juanita. Count to five hundred. I need time to get to the bushes -- the jungle."

I headed straight into the bushes along Ankeny, turned left, and quickly laid a false trail by hanging a few hairs on twigs; then I came back by another trail. But few trunks were big enough to hide behind and many shrubs were almost leafless. A fairly big evergreen loomed ahead. Climb it!

Settled firmly several branches up, I congratulated myself. I was high enough to see Roberta coming from any direction. So close to the trunk I probably wasn't quite invisible, but she probably wouldn't look upward to find me. As Juanita, I'd scooted up the tree to escape from marauding slave hunters....

Footsteps? Roberta entered the bushes. Swish, swish, slap went her stick against the bushes, louder and louder. I held my breath as she passed below, watched her tan sweater disappear....

Loud footsteps, low whistling: that big friend of Mose Baum's. Bobbo. As he stopped a few feet away, a patch of tan moved along the trail toward him. When the tan stopped moving, I clapped my hand over my mouth to keep from laughing. Would Juan, hearing but not seeing, dash in for a glorious reunion with Juanita?

What was Bobbo doing? Oh my goodness. He'd opened his pants, and was doing it right in front of me. Trapped between curiosity and embarrassment -- conflicting emotions! -- I took a good look, then closed my eyes tight while the splash of water whooshed on and on. Could I ever open my eyes again? Silence. What if he glanced up? Was that what the silence meant? No, thank stars. Now he was whistling softly, his footsteps fading away. I opened my eyes just in time to see him disappear into Ankeny.

Oh, wow. Roberta must be collapsing, holding in her laughter until we could explode together. But where was she? Only leaves stirred in her spot. Hadn't she seen us? I counted to a hundred before moving. A man-eating snake chased me down, Juanita would tell Juan, who must have headed for Thir-- down river. Pausing often to listen, I went to the end -- six blocks for me, six miles for Juanita. Halfway back my scalp prickled: Not a creature was stirring in the deep, dark, dangerous jungle.

Shivering, I shot out into the sunlight. As I ambled toward the pond, the Dailey boys overtook me. "Have you seen Roberta?"

"No. Have you seen the cops? They're supposed to come."

"No. What for?"

"Don't know yet. Some little girl maybe was kidnapped."

DORIE! I started running. People clustered in little groups, and yes, a policeman stood talking to a gray-haired man. Dorie Dorie Dorie ... and there she was, right where I'd left her.

I sank down on the bench, breathless. "Where's Rahtah?"

It took a minute for her question to sink in. Roberta? Could she be -- The benches were empty; I headed for the nearest group, near the bushes.

"PEGGY? PEGGY! SWEET JUMPING JESUS YOU ESCAPED."

Roberta ran towards me, tears streaming. We fell in a hugging heap. "I thought you were dead," she sobbed. "Or worse."

A policeman loomed over us. "Is this the missing girl?"

"Yes," she said, producing a fresh batch of tears.

Me? Missing?

"Can you tell us what happened? Describe the man?"

"What man?"

"The kidnapper," howled Roberta. "The man who ravaged you."

"But no one --"

"He chased you up a tree. I saw him there, threatening you. I ran for help, like we always planned, so he wouldn't get both of us, and a boy on a bike went to call the police, and --"

"Roberta, nothing --"

"Peggy, I saw you hiding up --"

"But I wasn't hiding from --"

"And I saw what the bad man was doing. PEGGY, HE WAS EXPOSING HIMSELF AT YOU."

"He was only...." Oh heavens above. Half a dozen policemen and a couple dozen people now surrounded us, listening to every word. I couldn't tell all those glowering grown-ups that I'd spied on a high-school boy while he urinated.

"Sorry, miss, but we have to ask you some questions. Are you calm enough to talk to us?" Calm? Of course I wasn't calm. So I served up my own batch of tears to prove it.

Two policemen drove us home. Crying, Dorie flew into Mother's arms; drying up, I flew upstairs, where I could watch them leave from our window. When Mother started up the stairs, I scrambled onto my bed, buried my face in my pillow. I got as close to truth as possible by shaking my head: Nothing bad happened to me, no man threatened me, I wasn't hurt, or even scared. "All right, child. You're home safe and sound, and nothing else matters."

Hopeless, I nosed deeper into my pillow. When they got to details, they'd notice we left the little girls alone, and then the whole world would find out how irresponsible we really were.

74

Oh Roberta.... What would happen to our precious and eternal best-friendship now?

"But you're the victim," said Roberta, furious again. "You have to go with me."

The police had asked us if we were willing to identify the child molester in a lineup. "I already said I would. But I told them and I've told you a hundred times I didn't see a bad man."

"You're a liar. If I saw him, you saw him."

"I did see someone. I saw a boy. A whistling high-school boy. He was just walking along, minding his own business."

It was my lie and I was stuck with it. I longed to tell her what I'd seen from the tree. In the old days it would have been easy. In my rehearsals it was easy. Quick to sympathize with my plight, she'd be quick to laugh with me.... But things went too far too fast. We weren't alone together for several days afterwards; by then we were so mad at each other we'd forgotten how to laugh. So I was also stuck with a double-barreled truth:

If it wasn't funny, it was a humiliating experience; if it couldn't be funny, it couldn't be told, even to Roberta.

Things got worse after the police closed the case "in absence of victim testimony." Everyone at school followed her around, begging for scary details. The bad man got bigger, blacker, fiercer every day. No one came near me, even after they heard how bravely I'd fought him off (yelling, kicking, punching, and cleverly shinnying up a tree whose branches wouldn't hold him) because I refused to say a single word. How could I mention Bobbo now? Or stand to make a bigger liar out of Roberta than she already was? Only my parents believed me anyway ... or, at least they didn't want to talk about it any more than I did.

One big relief: Nobody noticed that we'd failed our little sisters. Mother frowned halfheartedly, let it go. But Roberta and I were like Maggie and Jiggs; we couldn't spend two minutes together without scrapping -- mean, hurtful, nonstop scrapping that couldn't get out of its own rut.

"If I'm a liar, you're a snake in the grass," I said, without heat, as we walked home from school on the Wednesday before

Thanksgiving. I had high hopes for the holiday. Maybe, if we could stay out of each other's way for the whole four days, we'd start forgetting and would be back to normal by Monday.

"Phooey! I'm the one who saved your life, remember?"

"Double phooey! You're the one who doesn't know the truth when it bites her in the nose."

"You're the snake in the grass. Friends always back each other up in a pinch."

"Yeah? Well, there wasn't any pinch. We were just playing a game. And now thanks to you and your crazy kidnapper we'll never get to go to the park alone again."

"What do I care? We're going to move to the Heights over Christmas anyway."

I froze in my tracks. "Moving? I don't believe it."

She stopped too, and stomped her foot. "You better believe it. We bought that house near the girls."

"So fast?"

"It's not fast. My parents signed the papers while we were at camp, and sold ours a month ago."

"You didn't tell me."

"I didn't want to break your heart. That's when I was dumb enough to think we were best friends -- sisters for all eternity. Some sister you are."

Were there tears in her eyes? In mine? I ran for home.

Dorie, waiting on the porch, twirled me into her jingling, jumping, joyous jig. How did I manage to do that? I wondered, heading for Mother in the kitchen.

"Roberta's moving," I mumbled. "At Christmas."

"Oh dear. She finally told you." She looked at me long and hard. "Can you take it?"

I moved in closer for the hug I saw coming. "I'll miss her."

"You'll miss her terribly. We all will. She's been a wonderful little friend for you."

Like Father Barbour with his yes, yes, Fanny, we said no more about it. I'd planned to cry as soon as Dorie fell asleep, but found no tears available. Instead I found that a tiny little spark inside had grown into a warm fire: the strangely marvelous discovery that I hadn't been quite as alone in my balancing act as

I'd thought. Roberta, too, had been carrying around a heavy load of secrets and daily half-lies. So had Mother and Daddy ... and even the Northrups.

Was that what they meant by "common humanity"? This thought seemed pretty profound, so I sat up to probe it -- to enjoy the relief of knowing that at least things had to change now. Was this how a seal felt when the big slithery ball finally tumbled off his slippery little nose?

"Pah okay?" Dorie wasn't really awake, but I answered anyway. "Sure Pah's okay. I've dropped the ball, that's all."

I knew deep in my heart that Roberta and I had somehow failed each other miserably, and that I would miss her for the rest of my life. But everything had been so wrong, for so long, that it just had to be easier now. What's more, I wasn't going to mind at all getting my collecting hands on the P words.

No! Not yet! We still had several weeks to get through.

Sighing, I snuggled down for a comforting recital: roster, rhapsody, roughage, ruminate, rapport, roustabout, ramshackle, rejuvenate, raffish, rip-snorting, raucous, razzmatazz, repercussion, rub-a-dub-dub, Rumpelstiltskin... Rapunzel....

No! A valiant prince never cries. A valiant prince presses on purposefully.

Prevaricate, perpetual, perimeter, pettish, put-put, pique, pianissimo, pasteurized, pip, posthumous, polygamy, pulp, pester, precinct, pixilated, preposterous, propinquity ... propinquity ... propinquity....

VI.
BUTTERFLIES IN THE BASEMENT

Scan any newspaper and you'll find writers clambering onto a basement bandwagon: "Siberia, the basement of Russia"; "gutter language and basement logic"; "the basement team of the NFL." Obviously, sniff I, the five-rooms-on-a-slab building boom after World War II has now deprived several above-ground generations of any personal acquaintance with the word's actual geography -- its true location, nature, function, scope.

Although the Couch Street house had two stairways to the basement -- an outside one from the back, near the garage; an inside one from the central hall -- I went down neither for at least a week after we moved in. And that day I went down alone, to fetch a can of vegetables from a closet in the corner.

Dark stairs, dusty air, dead light from small, high windows viewing only dirty gray concrete.... "Spooky spooky spooky!" proclaimed the returning hero, brandishing the corn.

"Good girl. You've earned yourself a daily assignment."

Nobly, I shared my noble mission with Dorie. Hand in hand we crept down the stairs each afternoon at five-thirty.

"Boo!" Dorie whispered when a shadow lunged our way.

"Hsssst!" I hissed at the rustle of -- of what? "Begone! Be off! Be forever plunged into utter outer darkness." It was my own incantation, delivered with thundering ferocity.

Down the stairs, across the gloom to the central bulb; its eerily swinging light woke up beasts that loomed jaggedly in front and grabbed hungrily from the rear.

"Scat scat the cat!" shouted Dorie, holding tight with one hand and slashing the air with the other.

Into the faraway closet, and the slippery capture of the dangling bulb.... First the hoots and hugs, then the choice: peas; creamed or whole corn; spinach; sliced, quartered, diced, or pickled beets; french-cut, green, or yellow beans; stewed tomatoes; or sauerkraut. Dorie, a pushover for red, liked beets and tomatoes best. I chose the rollables -- peas and whole corn -- for the pleasure of the fork-in-hand chase. Mother required equal time for spinach. Daddy was indifferent for the most part but seldom finished his sauerkraut.

We took turns carrying back the can, the empty-handed one dowsing the lights from the rear. Because we'd carefully shut the hall door behind us, we sprinted up the stairs in blackness -- panting, screaming, exploding into the light with hundreds of hungry demons right on our tails.

"Why in heaven's name must you slam the door like that?" said Mother daily, but she never expected an answer.

Bit by bit the basement lost its fearsome charm. The neighborhood gang helped scrub and whitewash the walls; we played Tom Sawyer's fence as we worked, exulting in the mess. Every week a junk man took more clutter but we kept the treasures: a wind-up phonograph and a stack of squeaky records; magazines for cutting up; a wooden icebox with four doors; a sooty glass chimney welded by wax to a grubby dish. (Aladdin's wonderful lamp for sure.) By fall electricians had installed ceiling fixtures, wall outlets, and, at the top of the stairs, a three-switch plate. While Daddy worked on his Labor Day project, I sweated out my first poem:

> Daddy is painting the basement floor.
> It's black and shiny, and so is the door.
> He stenciled a border of red and green,
> With stripes of yellow in between.
> Now he's handsome as can be --
> He matches the basement to a T.

I circled "to a T," penciled in "or perfectly?" "Which is best?" I asked Mother.

"It's perfect as it is," she said, tacking it to a bulletin board at the bottom of the stairs. On the same wall, she made a large square with paper tape, filled it in with floor paint.

"Some blackboard," I said. "It's too shiny to take chalk."

She hung up a bull's-eye nearby, then hid the darts. "Too dangerous, I m afraid. You might knock each other's eyes out."

80

"Whose playroom is this anyway?" I grumbled.

All grumbling ceased as we explored the magic of the "raft" we found under the junk. If we centered it against a wall, presto! It was a stage for variety shows: singing, tumbling, tap dancing. If we put it in the middle, another presto: a desert island for Robinson Crusoe or Pegleg Pete, a sailing ship for Sinbad or Popeye, an ark for Noah, a canoe for Hiawatha, a whale for Jonah ... or, Dorie's favorite, a beautiful pea-green boat. If we tucked it into a corner, still another presto: a room for playing house, an Alpine hut for Heidi, a bleachers stand....

By the time winter arrived, bright lights and fresh paint had turned the basement into a spacious playfield, sheltered in the far corner by a spreading elm of a furnace, a branched, breathing guardian pretending to give shade. We gradually brought down old clothes, orange crates, dishes, bedding -- multipurpose props for play-acting, building material for houses and villages, equipment for picnics and camping out under our tree.

"This is <u>my</u> corner," said Mother, patting the washtubs beneath it. Her equipment too came gradually: a wringer washer; a network of overhead clotheslines; an ironing board "I never have to take down"; and, to our scorn, a shabby redwood picnic set "I stole off the junkman's truck for fifty cents."

"I have big plans for it," she said mysteriously when Daddy objected and I turned up my nose. "You'll change your tune."

A week later she invited us down for a tune-changing look. Lined along the back wall, topped with yellow-and-white checked oilcloth, the table had turned into a counter for a hot plate, the benches into a long, sunny landing spot for a copper canning kettle, wicker laundry baskets, pots of wintering geraniums. At one end the iceless icebox stood agape to display jars of fruit and jam. Daddy whistled a brand new tune, and so did we.

After school I often found her by following with my nose the wispy wafts of bleach, soap, melting paraffin, bubbling marmalade, and soaking cod for Christmas lutefisk. "It's the coziest spot in the house," she'd murmur in winter as she carried down Swedish coffee cake to rise near the furnace. "It's the

81

coolest spot in Portland," she'd murmur in summer as she trooped us down to help cap a batch of root beer.

Daddy's domain, much smaller, was directly catty-corner, near the canned-goods closet. He moved in a cardtable, a straight chair, a floor lamp, a typewriter, and several cartons of books and papers. Grandpa's "corner" -- an easel, a small rickety table for brushes, paints, jars -- chased after the best light when he was with us, disappeared when he left.

Though the basement was off limits when Daddy was writing, he never heard me tiptoe down. Dorie always knew where I was; too obedient to go down herself, she hovered at the door. "Either sneak down with me or go somewhere else," I pleaded. "Mother's going to catch on if you stand there."

"Doh helps Pah study from right here," she insisted, stubborn. "Doh never tells on Pah."

Glorying in those stolen hours, I read forbidden comic books, daydreamed, poured intrigue, exaggeration, and outright lies into my diary. "Today Harriet and I spent hours looking for a secret chamber -- rapping on every inch of wall," I wrote in 1934. In 1935: "The basement's a smoke-filled den of iniquity at night. Who knows what manner of evil lurks there while we lie snug in our beds?" In 1936: "Roberta and I smell something foul afoot in the vacant lot on Ankeny. Smugglers?" In 1937: "I think Daniel's finally grown tired of Mitzi. He chose me first for his prison ball team!!!!!!"

One summer weekend Daddy built a Ping-Pong table -- an early harbinger of a season of major transformation.

"Ping-Pong tables are green," I begged. "With white lines on them, for playing doubles. And they're never shiny."

"This one matches the blackboard."

It displaced Daddy's work corner; a sturdy new cardtable set showed up at the bottom of the stairs. While Daddy cruised Canadian forests, a carpenter enclosed Mother's corner -- about a fourth of the basement. Surprised by the darkening within it, she immediately had Sears install linoleum flooring: huge yellow buttercups and white daisies on a grassy green background.

As we admired it, her next idea flashed like a beam of sunlight: "Let's put up the hammock."

The new partition created a natural corner. Half grumbling and half laughing, the carpenter installed hooks. "Never heard of no one hanging a hammock in the washer room," he said.

Giggling, Dorie and I unfolded a couple of slingback canvas chairs that were standing against the wall for winter.

Mother clapped her hands. "We've made a plaza. Our very own plaza in our very own basement." Even the clotheslines agreed; when the furnace heaved a sigh, aprons and dishrags fluttered overhead like leaves and flowers in a gentle breeze.

"Or like butterflies," said Dorie, flitting across the green. "Doh's a pretty butterfly too."

Within months the rumpus-room craze hit Portland. When Daddy asked "Who on earth wants a rumpus in the basement?" three hands waved in the air. So while he visited Alaskan forests, workmen turned the end wall into a brick fireplace that shared the chimney with the front-room fireplace. While he was in Arkansas, the carpenter sheathed the partition and staircase with knotty pine, built a bar with a swinging door. I begged for a coke machine, to make it a real soda fountain. Ignoring my plaint ("Who wants coffee in beer mugs?"), Mother brought down the electric coffee pot and hung her collection of mugs on the wall.

"This is indeed one fine rumpus," admitted Daddy, as he drank coffee from a mug that looked like an old man's face. It was his pleasure, he said, to upgrade the painted floor. "But you can all help. We'll do it Thanksgiving weekend."

"Any ideas on the color?" Mother asked, showing us magazine photographs of rooms with floors of rubber tile.

"Doh takes red."

I chose powder blue; my new friend Lillian said blue was definitely my color. Mother leaned toward soft green. Daddy didn't know. "Brown?" We all laughed him down.

"What color? What color?" we asked the day she'd gone downtown to order them.

"It's a surprise -- to me, too. I got them at an unbelievable sale. As is, so I couldn't choose."

On Friday morning we assembled for work and for viewing. "Red red red," chanted Dorie, clapping.

With a grand flourish, Mother pulled out a tile. Brown. Even Daddy was disappointed. "No. Look. This one's yellow. Brown and yellow, I guess. Two colors."

It turned out to be the entire range. Scrawled on each box: "Misc. colors" and "NOT RETURNABLE." Ooohing and aaahing, Dorie pulled out slabs of red, blue, green, black, tan, brown, yellow, to arrange into patterns.

"That's why they were so cheap," Mother whispered. "I should have known better."

Daddy patted her hand. "It's okay, Anna," he said, and put us to work. I sorted them by size and color; Dorie picked out each tile; Mother spread the glue; Daddy pressed them down and wiped up the ooze. Finally Mother spoke: "It's lucky I had to buy three boxes too many. We can use less brown."

Was that a tear plopping down on the tar? Dorie was crowing too happily over each rainbow tile to notice that the sky might be falling. Every few minutes Daddy told us how beautiful it was, what a good job we were doing.

"That's no doubt the best tile in the world for this spot, Dorie. Look at that, everybody. What could be better?"

"Doh knows how to pick," she sang as she darted out and in to drop each tile into Mother's hand.

Roberta would have made fun of the jumble, I thought, hoping I liked it. Sitting back to squint, I finally decided that maybe I did. It was a rumpus room, after all, and could take a rumpus of color. "I like it," I said now and then, louder each time.

By noon Mother was squinting occasionally too. By nightfall she was laughing. "I can't believe it. It's perfectly beautiful -- a crazy quilt of colors."

On Saturday the neighborhood kids wandered in and out to admire the floor and to envy us. On Sunday Daddy let them help lay out the odd sizes for the edges.

"It's a giant's jigsaw puzzle," breathed Herbie.

A few days later the carpenter brought the hardware for the door and staircase. "Never saw a floor like that," he said.

"I got them on a wonderful sale. I think they're leftovers."

"Cheap, huh? Mind if I bring the missus to see it?"

"We've set our own style," Mother reported proudly at dinner.

We set our own style on the walls, too.

"Axel," said Mother, a few nights before Grandpa was due to arrive. "Axel, what do you think about letting Grandpa loose on the walls? A continuous mural?"

Daddy thought highly of it and Grandpa seemed oblivious to our wonder as Sweden flowed from his brush. Fields, mountains, trees, clouds, a lake ... a furry figure. Lassie?

"What's a dog doing there?" whispered Harriet.

"It's got horns, silly," said Alice. "Dogs don't have horns."

"A billy goat," said Herbie.

I nodded. "Or maybe a reindeer."

"Donder!" said Dorie.

"Or Comet, or Cupid, or --"

"It's a MOOSE!" bellowed Grandpa, and sent us packing.

"Vamoose, it's a moose!" I shouted as we burst outside.

"Vamoose, find a goose!" shouted Herbie.

"Vamoose, a moose and goose are loose!" shouted Harriet.

"Vamoose, a moose and a goose are loose in the hoose!"

"Oh, don't be so childish!" said Alice.

Too late. A new game was born.

Every Friday, Mother visited Meier and Frank's tenth-floor Dream House. Finally she found the "pioneer set" she wanted: a loose-cushioned couch, two easy chairs, a coffee table, and two end tables, all made of knotty pine with wagon-wheel details.

"Oh my goodness," I said when I saw it; we'd never before bought a whole roomful of furniture at once. Massive, colorful, inviting, it completely filled up the fireplace end, leaving no room for our stage/boat/house. "We're getting too big for it anyway," I added, not at all sure that it was so.

At my thirteenth birthday party, Mother led us to the basement for the unveiling of my present: a knotty pine desk, in place behind the bar. The next day, feeling ten feet tall, I invited Harriet and Alice in for "a pot of coffee in my new office."

Alice dressed for it; she wore a hat and gloves that she kept on while she was there. "Let's do this often," she said several times, sending her smile past me to Harriet.

"Let's not and say we did," said Harriet, still escaping from Alice's icky clutches.

Meanwhile, as Roberta moved out of my diary, Ping-Pong scores moved in, recording my rise to neighborhood champion. The first summer without her I wrote page after page of poetry, soon abandoning the lowlands of dale/vale to picnic on the plateaus of apostrophe/catastrophe and to scale such dizzying heights as weigh/bouquet/hooray. That fall I couldn't say enough about a classmate named Lillian Appleton.

"Why didn't we spot each other sooner?" I asked my diary, and often mused, "Except for her brown eyes, we could be twins" -- pretending that I too had naturally curly hair, slim legs, and a waist that already dipped in and out.

She lived fifteen long blocks away, so we spent hours on the phone. "Ten minutes, once a day," said Mother, exasperated. It was no real problem; Mother was often out of earshot.

We both took popular piano from Jerry Stone. Mother wouldn't let me take tap dancing with Lil at the Richard Billings studio, but she let me join his ballroom class at the Laurelhurst field-house with the rest of the neighborhood. I begged for a "real electric record player, so I can practice my lessons," and on Christmas morning there it stood, right next to the moose.

"But it's not your phonograph, miss greedy," said Mother, closing down four hours of "Deep Purple" and "Blue Evening."

Dancing class was on Thursday nights. "I didn't mind missing Henry Aldrich at all," said I to my diary. "Charles was soooo attentive." Another day: "I almost had to slap Daniel to keep him from getting fresh." In reality, I stumbled and sweated with sulky, chin-high boys for a long two hours. The fun came later, on the afternoons when Lil and I swayed together in the basement to "Polkadots and Moonbeams" -- eyes closed to better envision our own someday polkadot, moonlit splendor.

With the arrival of my desk I had full access to the basement. Lil came often to study; study meant lists. We listed sweaters, skirts, socks, ribbons -- exposing the need for matching items, so we could dress like twins. We listed each other's virtues, the virtues we valued in boys. Stifling laughter, we listed what we might say to the first boy who phoned, to the first boy who kissed us. Starry-eyed on everyone's behalf, we listed romantic partners: for skating parties, dances, the rumpus-room parties we would one day give, co-belles of any ball.

In creating the hospitable basement, was Mother dreaming too? My parents never used it in a social way themselves; did they hope I'd blossom into a Trixie-like teenager, pretty and peppy and popular, who drew popcorn parties to her door...? Shy, self-conscious, clumsy, no Rose of the Rumpus Room was I. At thirteen I bubbled into my diary, "Daniel admired my game, loved my dress." At sixty-nine I still wince at the painful memory of a Daniel who, trounced at Ping-Pong, threw his paddle at a Swedish mountain and stomped up the stairs. (Skedaddle the paddle!)

The sweet lies fed my heart, Lil filled it, but a heavy cloud hung over me: Mother's unshakable disapproval of Lil. "She's too sassy for her own good," she'd say; or "She brings out the worst in you"; or "She's a bad example. You'd never see Roberta in a skirt that short."

Would Mother ever get over losing Roberta?

Lil never looked humble, never bothered to lie, divert, or mislead; adults were big enough, she figured, to take her as she was. Without hesitation, and without telling Lil, at home I turned myself into a round-the-clock lie factory to account for the time I spent with her; under dozens of elaborate covers, I slinked out the front door to sally forth on our Adventures into Adolescence. We bicycled to Blue Lake, bused to Jantzen Beach, walked to the Shake Shop on Sandy, where the Grant High School kids hung out ... destinations that were not yet forbidden only because Mother hadn't yet thought of them as temptations.

"But I'm living on borrowed time," I whispered to Dorie at night. I dreaded the day when Lil would, inevitably and innocently, spill some disastrous beans. Meanwhile, if I couldn't ask Lil to lie, I could at least stash her in the basement, to reduce her opportunities for spilling.

Mitzi already had Grant friends; weak with admiration, we studied her every move. At last, in 1940, we started at Grant --a heady world of whisper-filled classes, lockerside trysts, sociable hallway parades, and endless study-hall lists filled with brand new people. Out of school I lived in pincurls and bandanas, buried my bra (which I had to stuff with tissue to make useful) in the cedar chest between wearings, praying that Mother never found my growing cache of Grant-girl booty: Tangee lipstick, an eyelash curler, school-passed notes, dozens of Woolworth's four-for-a-quarter strip photos of the two of us, black-lipped and sultry-eyed, in Betty Grable or Veronica Lake poses.

"We have to learn to flirt," said Lil, so we went to Friday afternoon mixers in the gym, and to all the school games. When she bought a white sharkskin tennis dress, I made one like it, the better to hang around courts, flirting with athletic boys.

"We have to learn to be stuck-up, too." That's what Grant girls were famous for; we puzzled for hours over the conflicting demands of growing up.

"Make new friends!" said Mother, over and over. "Grant must be full of wholesome girls like Roberta." And: "Can't you spend a single evening upstairs with us? I know full well you girls aren't studying down there." And I knew full well why we spent so many weekends at our Mt. Hood cabin: Mother was trying to pry me away from both Lil and basement privacy.

Her plot worked, temporarily. After summer school (I'd flunked algebra), we lived at the cabin for a month. Back in school, Lil and I made up for lost time by occasionally skipping a class. It was so easy that soon we were heading downtown -- to the movies, or to the shops to try on jewelry, or to the Rainbow Room for cokes -- a couple of afternoons a week. Since "school" was an automatic cover, I hardly noticed that I was living a lie.

With Pearl Harbor, the war came gently to Portland. Mother made blackout curtains for the basement; Daddy joined a car pool; the whole neighborhood hummed "God Bless America"; and Dorie and I shared the weekly wiggly chore of squeezing yellow coloring into a claylike sack of margarine. But within a few months I plunged into a far more devastating war of my own making.

The opening gun: I lost my purse one spring day at school. A helpful soul turned it in; a snoopy one read its contents, passed it on to my counselor. If the list of dates we'd skipped school wasn't enough to sink my ship, the attached details were: my romantic accounts of what we'd done. Two boys, P and S, showed up often, saying such things as "You're the maiden I've beheld in my dreams," and "Pray, do share with me your innermost thoughts, Pretty Little Miss Blue Eyes."

It was history's shortest war.

Mother shot down all attempts to tell her that P and S stood for Penrod and Sam, enlisted because they were more interesting (and much more interested in me) than any real boys around. I'd have welcomed a prolonged attack of small artillery but Mother said only, "I will not allow you to ruin your life because of bad company," then dropped two big bombs: I was never to see Lil again; and my life as a Grant girl was over.

Humiliated, heartbroken, furious, I sulked in the basement for the rest of high school -- as a day student at St. Helen's Hall, an Episcopal school for girls. For months I ached for Lil, writing long, mournful letters I didn't mail, filling my diary with imaginary events in our reunited lives. At meal after meal, Mother hardly spoke to me, Daddy seldom looked my way, and Dorie smiled timidly from face to face. Yeah, yeah, and yeah I said to her nightly Mah-Dah-Pah-okay? check. Though I knew she didn't quite believe me, I couldn't find the heart to help.

Neighborhood bonds had long ago loosened. Cora Jean, attending Commerce High, slipped into an alien country of steno pads and office jargon; Alice, purring about social acceptability, evaporated into a sorority sisterhood of smug superiority; Harriet, somersaulting between euphoria and despair, lived only for a boy named Tim. Like the self-possessed Hall girls, they had no time for a fallen warrior, and I hid my wounds from everyone.

On the nights I needed to cry -- swamped by the gulf between what I was and what I wanted to be -- I abandoned my bed for the basement hammock and the motherly murmuring of the furnace. If Dorie heard me leave, she padded down behind me to bed down on the couch. Separated by the partition, we couldn't hold hands but we could sing. I always fell asleep without my cry; Dorie was always gone by morning; and I always smiled as I pictured her brave return alone.

Even after I made some lukewarm friends at the Hall, I enjoyed hiding all pleasure, each small success, from Mother. And my falling grades still fed the fire; because Mother blamed my Grant ones on Lil, I had to prove I could do worse without her.

"What are you up to down here instead of studying?" asked Mother, appearing at my shoulder. The creaking stairs warned me just in time to cover my work; knowing she'd poke around when I wasn't there, I burned each letter immediately, hid my diary high on an arm of the furnace.

At some point, suddenly done with letters, I also leapt the blue leather fences of my diary -- not into reality, but onto reams of yellow paper that I populated with honestly fictional characters, separate enough from me to be cheerful. In a permanent daze, I walked in their shoes, thought their thoughts, captured their words, celebrated their happy endings, then burned each story with no regrets. I was no latter-day Jo March, hoping to publish her work; I was a Lone Adventurer, exploring an invisible and rewarding world, forever immediately at hand.

At some point too I had to accept as fact (confirmed by two biology books and the gym teacher) the rumor I'd scorned for years: that a male's appendage for urinating was not only his apparatus for depositing seed but also his weapon for rape. Holy cow, I muttered, shocked that God would design such a ridiculous mechanism. A still holier cow stampeded in immediately: That might explain Roberta's reaction in the park that awful day; in knowing something I hadn't known, she saw a danger I couldn't see -- a potentially real danger, not a wholly imaginary one.

Could I share the huge relief of my belated understanding? Would she, at long last, laugh with me at the embarrassing and only truth I saw from the tree? For days, whenever the house was empty, I headed upstairs to the phone. Finally I got as far as dialing; when her mother answered, I hung up.

Too late, I decided, remembering how miserable we'd both been the few times our mothers got us together after she moved. Instead, glowing in a rebirth of affection for her, I spent weeks probing on paper into the part knowledge (or ignorance) plays in individual views of reality.

Oh, wow -- profound!

The summer after my junior year I took typing at business school. World War II had now arrived in earnest. Portland teemed with strangers in khaki and navy blue; local boys disappeared into uniform by the hundreds. Miss Sarah, widowed early, joined the WAACs; Cora Jean married a soldier; Harriet eloped with her Tim, now a sailor. For a couple of years, even our basement resounded with sporadic wartime conviviality as, three times in a row, I fell in love with young military men. Gratefully in love; none lived up to Roberta in Mother's eyes, but at least she saw some good in them. All three marched off to other fields, our red-hot letters soon burned out ... but typing did not. When I heard that Roberta was at Smith, and, later, that Lil had married a Dailey boy, nostalgia and regret swept in only temporarily. Nothing could stem my flow.

Though Daddy's old typewriter had no return bar, my increasingly nimble fingers massaged my brain and loosened my tongue; ideas, thoughts, stories tumbled into the tidy but thrilling life of printed words. The day I toted Webster's downstairs, Mother toted it back. "Oh, no you don't, Miss Greta Garbo," she said. "The only time we set eyes on you is when you come upstairs to look up a word." She was laughing; and we laughed together when I bought a Collegiate out of an early paycheck.

As contentment set in, curiosity grew; to have anything worth saying I had to sharpen my sights, scratch the shallow, crumbly crust of my own half-baked opinions. It took a couple of years -- one at Meier and Frank's, facing the tedium of an undemanding job; one at junior college bringing up my grades -- but mourning was past and peace reigned in our home. In giving me a typewriter for my twentieth birthday, my parents gave me my wings. When I emerged from the basement, blinking, to go off to the University of Washington, I'd taken a good healthy bite of the lesson of my life: With Webster's in one hand, a Royal portable in the other, Miss Peggy the Profound Prober didn't have to be either the pulp or the packaging of her own puny pickle.

My parents sold the Portland house that spring, eventually settled in Seattle where they built a house on Lake Washington. It had a basement -- a cheerful, full-daylight one, born beautiful -- but it wasn't my basement. My basement, well over half a century later, continues to define itself: an ever-shifting arena for courting and mastering fears ... a seasonal park of erupting playfulness ... a demanding schoolroom for developing skills ... a lonely no-man's land hospitable to unarmed thoughts ... a warm, loamy field to nurture the tender and hugely complex growth of sisterhood, daughterhood, friendhood, selfhood ... a safe chrysalis where the black shrouds of yearning lies could naturally self-destruct, allowing the colorful butterflies of impersonal imagination to at last take flight.

So "Humbug!" say I to those who equate basements with gloomy sepulchres, shabby, surreptitious, and second class, and think they deal with truth. "Bah and humbug!" say I ... and I say it from the multichambered, multilayered, multisplendored basement of my dear old Couch Street heart.

92

AFTER WORDS

What took me so long? I wondered, rejoicing in every detail of college life. Then, one dark mid-November morning, everything froze. A photograph in a psychology book showed several children, smiling broadly, each with a face exactly like Dorie's. The caption read, "Mongolian idiots, who occur in all cultures, rarely reach adolescence." I almost stopped breathing.

Under mongolism, Webster's said: "A congenital malformation . . . in which the child has slanting eyes ... a large tongue, a short skull, and broad hands with short fingers." Dorie? Her eyes did slant, slightly. Were her hands broad, her skull short? One thing I knew: Whatever those children were, Dorie was too.

Library books told me more. Incapable of intelligible speech, they were lethargic, uncoordinated, with a lurching gait. Lack of memory gave them at best the IQ of eight-year-olds; the less afflicted were termed imbeciles or morons. Considering them gifts from their gods, primitives raised them as tribal wards. U.S. statistics were unreliable; parents often hid them away. Each book strongly recommended institutional care, emphasizing their short life span as if it were a golden promise.

I'd realized that Dorie was "different," but so what? No one was like anyone else; some were more different than others, that was all. Take fun-loving Benny, almost an elf, and pale, quiet Crawford, isolated by genius; he lived with his piano teacher and practiced six hours a day. So her nonconformity was no problem. It was the label that rocked me. It robbed her of her personal uniqueness by dumping her into a scientific category, an icy box of doom, that my parents had kept secret from me.

Had everyone else known? Did Aunt Hannah know when she yelled that God was punishing my parents with Dorie? "For doing what?" I'd asked, intrigued. When she bit her lips, flounced away, I'd been pleased to catch a grown-up in a lie she couldn't prove.... Had all those giggling, self-satisfied high school girls known when they regularly cornered me with little moron jokes? Rotten packs of beasts; it served them right that I hadn't caught on.

But Dorie didn't lurch or babble. She was dainty, vivacious, graceful, sensible ... wasn't she? Though I hadn't planned to go home for Thanksgiving, I took a late bus Wednesday. Mother, oddly, didn't cheer at the news; I wasn't cheering either.

Dorie met me at the door for a short whirl -- limper, chunkier, clunkier than I remembered. She fell asleep fast on our songs. "Pah's home," she grinned on waking, then plodded to the table for a silent day of coloring. "No," she said, whenever I invited her to the park, or to the drugstore for ice cream.

"Is Dorie feeling okay?" I asked Mother as I wiped dishes.

She stopped washing to stare. "Of course. Why do you ask?"

"She seems so ... lethargic. She used to dance all the time."

"She's growing up. Like you. SHE'S NOT A CHILD ANYMORE."

Why was she shouting? I wanted to shout back -- that she was too a child, a forever child, dying daily. Instead, I fled to the basement, where I turned the record player high, higher, higher, tempting Dorie to join me. She didn't.

Sunday afternoon, alone on the bus seat, a terrible question roared in my head, heart, stomach: HAD I MADE MY DORIE UP?

When I came home for Christmas, Dorie was gone.

"Gone? What do you mean she's gone?"

"It's good news, Peggy. We've finally found a school for her," said Daddy, completely failing to look triumphant.

I burst into grateful tears. Dorie hadn't died without me.

"Peggy, she was so proud of herself," said Mother, crying too. "Over and over, it was 'Doh goes to school. Doh's big like Pah.' "

"There there," murmured Daddy, hugging us both. "It's okay."

It wasn't. My room was hollow; mealtimes were painful; Christmas was agony. IMITATION CHEER, my fury howled.

Can't we _ever_ be honest? "Can't we visit her?" was all I dared ask.

"Not yet. The school discourages visits for a while."

IT'S NOT A SCHOOL, fury bellowed. IT'S A LOONY BIN. Books told me the awful truth -- why couldn't they? And why couldn't I tell them what I knew, ask for more answers? I knew why: Their new fragility terrified me.

In June they sold the house; with Daddy consulting for several companies, I spent my holidays wherever they were. Ashamed of my cowardice, raging at their betrayal, I donned courtesy, secretiveness, boredom like a shabby overcoat. We seldom spoke of Dorie, and they resisted visiting her until my senior year. She was a couple of hours from Seattle, at the state institution at Buckley -- called, to my humbled surprise, Rainier School.

For a wrenching moment, in the office, she didn't recognize me; then she let out a big whoop and danced me out the door. In the car she held my hand, chanting "Pah sees Doh in school."

We settled on a bench in a nearby park with cones. "Doh goes to school," she said when her ice cream was gone.

"Yes," I smiled. "Dorie's a big girl. She goes to school."

Frowning, she stood up. "Doh goes to school _now._"

Daddy stood up too. "Okay, we'll go back." Without another word, she shot out the second we drove up. "Did you see the wind streak by?" asked Daddy. "That was our Dorie, checking in."

The receptionist laughed. "It's her story hour, you know."

Mother eventually caught my eye in the mirror. "Peggy, let's be grateful she's happy there. It's hard I know ... it's even worse if we try to bring her home. She starts crying in the car."

"I can't believe it. Doesn't she miss us? _Need_ us?"

"We don't know. The doctors say many act that way. One theory is they're sulking -- punishing their families for going away."

"They're nuts. Dorie _never_ sulks. She'd _never_ punish anyone for _anything_. _She's_ _just_ _too_ _good_ _to_ _hold_ a _grudge_." I'd leaned forward, to slap the front seat with every word.

In the sudden silence, I met Daddy's eyes in the mirror --
fond, amused, pleased. Mother's lips trembled in a half smile.
Oh dear God how I've missed them! I sank back, smiling
weakly, astonished: We'd somehow made it back to each other
again.

After graduating I lived in California for years, moved to
Hawaii in 1962. When I was home we didn't visit Dorie. "She's
forgetting us," said Mother. "It's best, I guess." She had tears in
her eyes when she said Dorie had lost all her teeth; and again, in
the midfifties, when she said Dorie no longer talked. "No one
knows why." Towards the end they visited her only at
Christmas. "But she doesn't respond, even to Santa."

Daddy died in 1965, Mother in 1968. In her last December,
as we wrapped Dorie's gifts for mailing, Mother absentmindedly
opened up. "I'm so glad you didn't see what happened when you
left. She didn't dance, sing, smile. Just faded away overnight.
That first Thanksgiving -- remember when you asked if Dorie
was sick? I was scared to death you'd caught on, might feel you
had to stay home to help. But there was no helping her ... and
we just couldn't let you go down into your black hole again."

Did I hug her? Oh dear, I suppose not. I remember all hugs.

After Mother died, Victor and I headed straight for Dorie --at
Hollycrest, a rambling house in Snohomish. I knew she'd talk to
me. No. She let us each take a hand for a walk, but showed no
recognition, no pleasure, nothing. A few days later she
disappeared within moments; I found her in her room, sitting us
out. I returned to Hawaii in tears for my whole lost family.

Reports came often: when she moved to nearby Merry
Haven for nursing care; when she stopped walking; when she
had cataract surgery.... She's in loving hands, I thought,
whenever they wrote or phoned. In November 1991 a call came
from Cathy Lindsay, a cheerful young woman paid from Dorie's
personal funds to take her on occasional outings. Her news:
Dorie's account was fat enough to bring me for a visit. Rather
huffily, I said I wouldn't consider spending Dorie's money, and
that we'd been discouraged from visits on leave-well-enough-
alone grounds.

"Let's have her come to us," said Victor that night, sending me into a tizzy. "Wonderful," said Merry Haven's Mary Stackpole. "Family visits always bring rewards." I read the turnabout as a nod of approval from my parents.

Just one sign, I prayed at the airport; please, one heartwarming sign that our Portland days still lived within her. A neat, still, silent little being in a wheelchair, she kept her eyes half closed, focused on an inner view -- of what? Cathy, Victor, and I took turns feeding her, cheering when she showed interest in the next bite. Hoping to light up a memory, at meals and at bedtime (she and I shared a room), I belted out our childhood songs and hymns. Not a single flicker the whole week. BUT: Whenever my hand landed near hers -- in the car, at the table, across the beds -- she grabbed it and hung on until she dozed off. And that was heartwarmth enough.

Merry Haven called in mid-January: Dorie was in intensive care with pneumonia at an Everett hospital. A week later an exultant nurse announced her return; from then on quavery-voiced ones reported her daily failure. Dorie died on February 9, 1992 -- an affectionate, joyful, unmixed blessing in our Portland years, a haunting mystery for the next half century.

So I ruminate, but no longer on my parents' betrayal. That issue dissolved decades ago, as I glimpsed the lonely heroics of their decisions: to raise their daughters together, then set them firmly on separate paths. They paid an unspeakable, unspoken-of price to send the bigger one -- the one who sassed, whined, lied, deceived, disobeyed, stole, raged, hardened her heart against them -- out into the world unencumbered.

Now I ruminate on the mystery of Dorie, with her steady parade of losses: Portland, family, teeth, speech, legs, eyes ... and surely the greatest of these is speech. How can one live without words, without a bridge to others, to one's own thoughts? For years I've joked that I don't know what I think about anything until it pops out of my mouth or typewriter. It's not a joke, nor is it always easy. I spend hours chasing a single idea, emotion, reaction, insight -- draft after draft, from angle after angle -- till it clarifies into the full color of something worth keeping, a truth to cherish. That's how I clean out the clutter that rattles around inside, disturbing the peace.

Did Dorie find another way? Did she deny words entry as well as exit? In keeping out definitions, nuances, associations, all memories and built-in emotions, was she able to distill her tiny private world into simple color, music, tranquility? Into pure, unreachable, heartbreaking sinlessness?

Could I, should I have -- "Oh for Pete's sake, child, don't push so," says Mother, still in there pitching.

So while I shelter in obedience, in tending to my own knitting miss, I secretly soar off on a butterfly's wings to find my big-little sister Dorie -- forever dancing in a vast orchard of treetops to a resounding chorus of "Rah rah rah for Doh."

POSTSCRIPT FROM PARADISE

It's late afternoon and the tradewinds are ideal for windsurfing. My teenage buddy Graham, with his rainbow-colored sail, must be out there waiting for me.

"Make way, make way -- here comes the grizzled grandfather of all windsurfers," I yell, and let out a few yodels for the sheer joy of living. But nobody's around to notice my not-so-youthful exuberance -- the same exuberance and euphoria all windsurfers experience as we follow our bliss into the wide blue yonder. In a state of natural high, we merge and become one with the elements. It's life at its most intense and, paradoxically, at its most contemplative. Go figure!

Well, I didn't find Graham that afternoon, but I did run into something totally unexpected.

Diamond Head to my left, Koko Head to my right, Aina Haina hills straight ahead.... When I reach the area where I scattered the last of Dorie's ashes, I remember the sweet short ceremony on the pier. Laughing and crying, Peggy sang all the verses of "Jesus Loves Me," threw leis in the water as we took off with Dorie's ashes. Kathy and her son Zack, in a kayak, paddled over the reef, the first relay. Then Graham and I took over on windsurfers, going far out to sea, with Dorie leaping into the winds, the waves, and the ocean spray. "Free at last, free at last" I swear I heard her singing above the booming surf.

Every time I'm out here now I think of Dorie, and the cosmic injustice inflicted upon her: the Down's syndrome that gave her an extra chromosome in each cell. The brain accepts the medical verdict meekly enough, but the heart rebels at nature's cruel programming. Did she notice that her mind and body betrayed her in early adulthood? Did she intentionally turn inward, ignoring her body ... or did her body stop obeying her mind ... or did her mind just stop giving orders, going slowly to sleep?

"I know you're out here somewhere, Dorie," I say aloud, just as a commotion erupts on the horizon. Dolphins at play? Let's take a closer look. When a large gray rock suddenly looms ahead, I have a hard time braking -- by dropping my sail and sitting down fast. It's not a rock. A tiny dorsal fin ... a bulky body . . . then a massive head emerges, almost within reach, the huge eye giving me a friendly appraisal. Was that a wink? "Friendly giant, friendly giant," I murmur, mantra-like, frozen in place.

The head slowly sinks, followed by the rest of the body, the tail waving a parting aloha, much like our trained dolphins at Sea Life Park. Silence. Will it come back?

Then comes the voice, like singing, or a musical instrument, high-pitched, feminine. "Doh's a whale now."

I have no trouble believing it. A girl who knew, yesterday, how to be a monkey, a butterfly, even the wind, can be anything she wants to be today: a whale, a dolphin, a friendly shark, a flying fish, or maybe an iwa bird. How about a big, fast-moving cloud or tradewind? And don't forget our Hawaiian rainbow.... "Oh, my sweet sister-in-law, welcome back! When my time comes, I'd love to join you and your playmates for some serious fun and games. Who wants to be a celestial couch potato?"

I rush home to tell Peggy that Dorie's out playing in another park -- our own aquatic playground, Maunalua Bay.

-- **Victor Pavel**

IN MEMORIAM

Peggy Brandstrom Pavel, 1926-1999

On December 7, 1996, Peggy and I went to the Honolulu Academy of Arts Christmas Fair. She complained of headache and dizziness. "Home," she begged. Fifteen minutes later, back in our driveway, she was out cold. I had to carry her in, laid her on the couch, and called 911. The paramedics arrived in minutes, administered first aid, and carried her to the ambulance on a stretcher.

In the Straub Emergency Room the diagnosis was that Peggy had suffered stroke. But I was not to dispair, because a new miracle drug, tPA, was available.

A week in intensive care, followed by stomach surgery for tube feeding, on to rehab, and finally home...all in 41 days. Though Peggy had lost her speech (aphasia), she could still sing, a good omen I thought. And so we sang all the way home on that beautiful morning of January 17th, full of optimism for the future.

For the next 8 months her life was very busy with daily therapies: physical, enabling her to learn to walk again; occupational, so that she could use her left hand (her right hand was useless); and speech, the hardest to master. Progress was encouraging on all fronts until one day in September when Peggy was suddenly stricken with seizures, painful and scary spasms lasting 3 to 10 minutes each. These persisted for more than a year, striking 2 to 3 times a week. Despite more tests and more medication, she gradually lost her will to exercise or attend her speech therapy classes at the University Medical School.

From the time of her stroke, Peggy's vocabulary was limited to a few words: "ho ho ho"; "yes, but"; and "oh my goodness." In the hospital she invented a new word, "BASHT," and used it effectively to express disapproval.

When I greeted her with "Hi, Peggy," she would reply promptly but unpredictably by saying "Hi, Virginia" or "Hi, Victor." When asked her name she'd reply "Brandstrom" without hesitation.

Despite all of her problems she was mostly cheerful and good humored, rarely cranky. Often when I'd come to see her in her bed after a short absence, she would say "Oh, oh, oh, oh!" with great joy and surprise in her voice, as if she'd never expected to see me again. When I sang my greeting, "Oh my darling," she would join in and we would sing the popular song together until I ran out of lyrics. Then it was time for a hug, a kiss, and a cuddle.

One night Peggy's screams woke me up. She was flexing the fingers of her right hand – paralyzed by stroke for two months – admiring them, laughing, beside herself with joy. Alas, the miracle didn't last. The revived nerves soon went back to sleep, turning her hand into a rigid claw, and our hopes into dust.

One morning, to cheer her up, I knelt in front of her and begged, "Peggy, will you marry me?" Her eyes widened, a big smile, girlish giggles, and she was happy all day long. A cheap trick, perhaps, but it worked time and again. We created our own quality time.

Peggy spent her last 6 months in a wheelchair or in bed. The seizures had taken their toll, both mentally and physically. How long could this go on? Friends advised me to check out some nursing homes. "Over my dead body," said her loyal hubby, fearing that the final decision might be made without his consent.

The end came suddenly. During an early dinner on June 19th, 1999, she had no appetite, coughed a bit, and pointed toward her bed. By the time I wheeled her to the bed she was gone. Again, I dialed 911, bringing paramedics reinforced by firemen. But this time, mercifully, our friend and neighbor Dr. K. arrived, took control, and officially pronounced Peggy dead. I told him about our membership in the University of Hawaii Medical School Body Donor program. He made a phone call, and a couple of young men came with a stretcher. Silently, reverently, they wrapped my Peggy in two long sheets and carried her out to their van. I followed in a daze--and bawled.

In March the U.H. Medical School sent me an invitation to attend Peggy's memorial service on April 1st. Many of our local friends and several from the mainland came to celebrate Peggy's life.

I brought her ashes home and scattered them in Maunalua Bay, as I had Dorie's eight years earlier. Deep in thought, meditating on the mysteries of life and death, scattering leis and Peggy's ashes, I recalled Dorie's "Free at last" triumphant shouts. What's this? "Speech at last!" Did I hear right? Speech at last? It made sense when I recalled Peggy's saying, and

103

writing, that of Dorie's many losses, speech was surely the greatest. Right, Peggy–and Dorie, too–"Speech at last, free at last, free speech at last." Rah rah rah, for Doh and Pah.

–**Victor Pavel**

Dorie and Peggy—The book

Peggy started writing what she called her "two books in one" about a decade ago, in alternating chapters; one half was autobiographical, covering her childhood and adolescent years, while the other half was based on her career as a writer and editor. The book's title was revealing: "My Love Affair with Webster's."

She had just mailed a few copies of her manuscript to mainland publishers when the stroke felled her, sparing her the pain of the rejection slips. Now the burden was on me. What to do? The traditional publishers apparently weren't willing to go along with Peggy's unorthodox concept of two books in one. To publish her original opus would have required time-consuming bibliographic research of the extensive extracts from other published works and permission from their copyright holders. "I'm not long for this world," I kept mumbling to myself after losing Peggy. So I decided to go ahead with "Dorie and Peggy" (my title), the autobiographical portion of her book, and worry about the other half later. The new technologies of "print on demand" and "e-publishing" came to my rescue in the nick of time.

Axel Brandstrom, my father-in-law, a forester, college professor, and author of forestry books, would no doubt approve of this publishing revolution: it saves trees in a big way. I have fond memories of him, especially his sense of humor. He used to make fun of our accents—both of us being foreign-born—by saying, laughingly, "Vell, vell, Wic" or calling me "Torvic," thus turning me into an instant Norseman. According to Peggy, he had read the big Webster's Dictionary (all 3,500 pages and 600,000 definitions) three times, cover to cover!

Anna, my mother-in-law, used to pay me the ultimate compliment by saying, "If you want something done right, let Victor do it." Coping with her two daughters, one sassy, gifted, and precocious and the other mentally challenged, must have been a superhuman task. She passed away in 1968, at home asleep in bed, as had Axel three years earlier. The rest of us should be so lucky.

Peggy's writing talents were legendary. I still hear from some of her friends who have been saving her letters for decades. They deserve a reward for their loyalty: a copy of "Dorie and Peggy," I often told myself. Her childhood playmates, too, will savor the long-ago events in Peggy's own inimitable words. Include our friends and relatives and we have a legion of avid readers.

Peggy loved to talk about her childhood. In fact, many episodes in her book were familiar to me anecdotally. Take her Grandpa for example. I used to question her apparently irrational dislike of the old man. "Surely he had *some* good qualities," I'd say in his defense. "I've never met a Swede I didn't like." In a moment of weakness—or maybe just to get me off her back— she finally opened up and revealed a secret. Yes, there was a scary, traumatic incident involving her and her Grandpa when she was a child. It seems she had a habit of making a trip to the bathroom in the middle of the night with her eyes closed. On that fateful night she proceeded as programmed, sat down, and opened the floodgates, thereby awakening her Grandpa who happened to be sitting beneath her. Peggy screamed and ran. Grandpa yelled and swore in Swedish. Dorie joined the chorus. Axel and Anna came running, expecting a bloodbath or worse. The entire house was in utter turmoil. There was no way for Peggy to reconcile with her Grandpa, or vice versa, from then on.

And yet I admired the old curmudgeon, especially for his artistic talents. He taught himself to paint and left a gallery of murals in each of his children's homes, besides a stack of framed oil paintings—all landscapes. Peggy inherited a number of these when her parents died and promptly gave them all away, mostly to her Seattle-area cousins. Over the years since then we've heard from Sweden that John Brandstrom's paintings of "the American Wild West" are very much in demand in his native country.

So hang on to your Brandstrom heirlooms, all you mainland cousins, while you enjoy reading your cousin Peggy's book.

As for me, it has been a joy, a heartbreak, and a labor of love to see her manuscript progress and mature into a published book. Now, let the rest of the world know and admire my Peggy, too.

–Victor Pavel

ABOUT THE AUTHOR

Born on March 18, 1926, in Bellingham, Washington, Peggy grew up in Portland, Oregon, with her sister Dorie. She graduated from the University of Washington in 1950 with a BA in creative writing, followed by short stint in graduate school at Stanford University. While still an undergraduate she was a guest editor of *Mademoiselle* (1948) and assistant editor of *Interim,* a regional literary magazine. She began her full-time employment at *Sunset* magazine in 1953, first in the advertising department, then as assistant to the editor-in-chief, and finally as copyeditor of the food-and-garden section until 1962. That year she moved to Hawaii, where she accepted the position of assistant editor at *Paradise of the Pacific* magazine; by the time she left the publication three years later she had become the managing editor. Peggy then turned to freelancing for Ortho Books and Horticultural Publishing, also writing a style manual for Regensteiner Press. After "retirement" in 1985, she worked for many years as the volunteer editor of the Lyon Arboretum newsletter and the Hawaii Stitchery and Fibre Arts newsletter. She suffered a stroke in December, 1996, and passed away in June, 1999. Her loving husband, Victor, has seen her book through to publication as a lasting tribute to her memory. Proceeds from the sale of this book will be donated to the National Down Syndrome Society, 666 Broadway, New York, NY 10012.